Aunt Ruth Grammar Drills for Excellence II

Answer Key

A Workbook Companion to

Aunt Ruth: The Queen of English and Her Reign of Error

by

Joel Schnoor

Gennesaret Press
202 Persimmon Place
Apex, NC 27523

www.gennesaretpress.com

COPYRIGHT © 2018 Joel Schnoor. All rights reserved.

ISBN: 978-0-9997343-1-5

Printed in the United States of America
Apex, North Carolina

Front cover illustration by Doug Oglesby
Interior art by Joel Schnoor

Terms of Use: The following copyright privileges are granted for use of this document:

1. *Copies may be made of this document for use within one individual family.*

2. *For use in a classroom setting (public, private, middle school, high school, university, or home school cooperative), copies may be made for one classroom. Making copies for an entire school or school district is prohibited.*

3. *Other permissions may be obtained by writing Joel Schnoor at joel@joelschnoor.com.*

4. *This document may not be resold. Any media containing this document may not be resold.*

Table of Contents

Lesson	Topic	Page
1	Than	7
2	Into or In To	8
3	Gerunds	9
Review 1		10
4	Go Went Gone	11
5	Myself	12
6	Superlatives	13
7	An Honor, a Hawaiian	14
Review 2		15
8	Bring and Take	16
9	Used To	17
10	Only Sentence Placement	18
11	Sentence Adverbs	19
12	Metaphors and Similes	20
13	Borrow, Lend, and Linking Verbs	21
Review 3		22
14	Adjectives and Adverbs	23
15	Verbs Ending in -t	24
16	Double Negatives	25
17	Passed and Past	26
Review 4		27
18	Numbers	28
19	Fragments	29
20	Transitive Verbs	30
21	Active and Passive Voice	31
22	Intransitive Verbs Rule!	32
23	Moods of Verbs	33
24	Simple Past, Present, and Future Verb Tenses	34
25	Past Participles	35
26	Perfect and Progressive Verb Tenses	36
27	Subjunctive Verbs	37
Review 5		38

Table of Contents (Continued)

Lesson	Topic	Page
28	Bad and Badly	39
29	Comma Splice and Sentence Fusion	40
30	More Commas	41
31	Colons and Semi-colons	42
Review 6		43
32	Etc.	44
33	Either Or, Neither Nor	45
34	Plurals	46
35	That, Which, Who, and Double Subjects	47
36	Double Possessives	48
37	Nonplussed, Whoever	49
38	Bored	50
39	Ellipses	51
40	Breath, Drier, and Lightning	52
41	Synonyms, Antonyms, and Homonyms	53
Review 7		54
42	Got	55
43	Possessives with Appositives	56
44	Let's, Less, and Fewer	57
45	A Veritable Cornucopia of Useful Information	58
Review 8		59

Comprehensive Review, Part 1 60
Comprehensive Review, Part 2 61
Comprehensive Review, Part 3 62
Comprehensive Review, Part 4 63
Comprehensive Review, Part 5 64
Comprehensive Review, Part 6 65
Comprehensive Review, Part 7 66
Comprehensive Review, Part 8 67
Comprehensive Review, Part 9 68
Comprehensive Review, Part 10 69
Comprehensive Review, Part 11 70
Comprehensive Review, Part 12 71
Comprehensive Review, Part 13 72
Comprehensive Review, Part 14 73
Comprehensive Review, Part 15 74

Lesson 1

Than

For each sentence, write the two ways the sentence could be interpreted.

A) with *than* as a conjunction, and B) with *than* as a preposition.

Example: I like eggplant more than you.

A) I like eggplant more than you like it.

B) I like eggplant more than I like you.

1. My coach wants me to jump higher than a kangaroo.

A) My coach wants me to jump higher than **a kangaroo jumps.**

B) My coach wants me to jump higher than **the height of a kangaroo.**

2. Margie was delighted to discover that she could roast a turkey four hours faster than Grandma.

A) Margie was delighted to discover that she could roast a turkey four hours faster than **Grandma can.**

B) Margie was delighted to discover that she could roast a turkey four hours faster than **she can roast Grandma.**

3. Michelangelo enjoyed painting ceilings more than Aunt Ruth.

A) Michelangelo enjoyed painting ceilings more than **Aunt Ruth enjoyed it.**

B) Michelangelo enjoyed painting ceilings more than **he enjoyed painting Aunt Ruth**

4.   Consider: Aunt Ruth found that she could lick an envelope faster than *him*. Using the object pronoun *him* forces *than* to be a preposition. Thus, this sentence can only mean *Aunt Ruth found that she could lick an envelope faster than she could lick him.*
If what we really intend to say is that Aunt Ruth could lick an envelope faster than this other person could lick an envelope, what pronoun should we use to replace *him* so that *than* is a conjunction? **Answer: he**

5.   Alice pointed to Eva and said, "I can eat an egg faster than _____."

If Alice can eat an egg faster than Eva can, should she use *her* or *she*? **she**

If Alice can eat an egg faster than she can eat Eva, should she use *her* or *she*? **her**

Lesson 2

Into or In To

Underline all errors of "into" or "in to."

"You won't believe who I ran <u>in to</u> today," Aunt Ruth said with a smile. Before I could wager a guess, she said, "You'll never guess, so before you put all your energy into it, let me tell you. I ran <u>in to</u> Herman."

"I don't believe it. I thought you were driving to the gym so that you could go in to work out. I'm surprised that you ran <u>in to</u> Herman. Who's Herman anyway?"

"Who's Herman? Who's Herman? You're asking me who's Herman?"

"Yes, that's correct," I replied.

"Well, I'm not sure. I was hoping you knew. I checked the contact list in my phone, and he's not there—I never added anyone with that name <u>in to</u> my contacts. Anyway, he says he knows you."

"I am entering into a befuddled state," I sighed.

"You are entering into the Befuddled Zone?"

"Yes, I am entering <u>in to</u> the Befuddled Zone."

The doorbell rang and a man stepped into the room. "I have come <u>into</u> see you, my long-lost friend," he said. "My name is Herman, Herman Waxenshine."

"Do I know you?" I enquired.

"Think back, deep into your past."

"My memory's not so good. I can't look <u>in to</u> my past any further than, oh, a week ago Tuesday."

"Good enough. Do you remember what happened that day?"

"Certainly. I walked <u>into</u> order an artichoke salad at Olivia's Deli on Green Street. It was delicious—fresh garlic had been blended in to enhance the flavor—so I ordered another to take home. Hmm, I don't remember bringing it in to put in the refrigerator."

"Exactly," said Herman Waxenshine. "I come <u>into</u> bus tables at the deli every Tuesday afternoon, and I noticed that you left without it. Here it is. It took me a while to find you."

He held up a box of moldy artichoke salad.

"Guess I'll have to stop <u>into</u> buy another salad," I sighed.

Lesson 3

Gerunds

Find the gerunds in the story below:

"<u>Laughing</u> is so important to happiness," he said, musing quietly to himself. <u>Watching</u> the children outside had reminded him of his youth, and he noticed how the children seemed really good at <u>encouraging</u> and <u>supporting</u> each other. "What do you think, Elmer?" the man suddenly asked, looking at his friend on the bench beside him. "Is <u>laughing</u> important for ducks too?"

"I'd say," said Elmer, "that in the grand scheme of things, <u>quacking</u> is more important than <u>laughing</u> for a duck."

"Why do you say that?" asked the man.

"Well, I would think that <u>shaking</u>, or <u>trembling</u>, or <u>fainting</u>—or at least <u>swooning</u> in some kind of distressful manner—would be more important to us water fowl. Frankly, I am not seeing that duck stew is reason for a source of <u>laughing</u>."

"Duck stew?"

"You said, 'Is <u>laughing</u> important for duck stew?'"

"No, I said, 'Ducks—COMMA—too,' not 'Duck stew.'"

"Oh, well, I didn't hear your comma. The <u>pronouncing</u> of punctuation has never really been your strong suit."

"And <u>commenting</u> on how we say things apparently is one of yours?"

"<u>Criticizing</u> is not part of my natural biome."

"Anyway, what are you thinking that my strong suit is?"

"<u>Wearing</u> that coat of armor that stands in the front hallway is your strong suit, I think. Nothing can pierce that coat of mail. Hey, what ... what are you doing? Why are you putting on those ice skates?"

"<u>Skating</u> has always been one of my favorite hobbies. I love seeing playing children. <u>Playing</u> with kids sounds like a great thing to do right now. <u>Sliding</u> back and forth on the ice will be good exercise. Yes, I am skating today. I will be laughing, too. Meanwhile, I think you should stand under the sink faucet and turn it on."

"Turn on the faucet? Why?"

"<u>Rolling</u> water off your feathers is one of your strong suits. <u>Practicing</u> that would be good for you."

"I think you're going quackers," sighed Elmer.

Review 1

Select the appropriate word.

1. **Consider this sentence:** I like tennis more than Herb.

   A) If I mean that I like tennis more than I like Herb, then I am using **than** as a conjunction / <u>preposition</u>.

   B) If I mean that I like tennis more than Herb likes tennis, then I am using **than** as a <u>conjunction</u> / preposition.

2. Eleanor thinks that eating a bowl of ice cream is easier than her dog.

   A) If **than** is a conjunction here, we mean that Eleanor thinks that eating a bowl of ice cream is easier than <u>her dog thinks eating a bowl of ice cream is.</u>

   B) If **than** is a preposition here, we mean that Eleanor thinks that eating a bowl of ice cream is easier than <u>eating her dog.</u>

Underline the correct word(s).

3. I ran <u>in to</u> / into see if the flowers had come yet.
4. King Henry VIII bumped in to / <u>into</u> Anne Boleyn, and the rest is history.
5. Janette drove in to / <u>into</u> town on her horse, but the bad guys had fled.
6. I'm a bit flustered because my mom says I'll turn in to / <u>into</u> an ogre if I stay up past midnight!

Underline any gerunds in the following sentences.

7. No, that's not a sandhills crane. Larry is practicing his <u>whistling</u> this morning.
8. The bat is flying across the room!
9. The [1]flying bat was not a threat, but the <u>flapping</u> of wings in the middle of the night had always disturbed Athena.
10. <u>Reading</u> and <u>writing</u> well are two tremendous skills to have.
11. The frog was leaping halfway across the pond!
12. Aunt Ruth was swaying to the music, enjoying the <u>soothing</u> of the ocean breeze, when she inadvertently stepped on Mr. Bunstable's poodle.

---

[1] This can be confusing, but *flying* is used as an adjective here and not a noun.

Lesson 4

Go Went Gone

Choose the correct verb form.

1. I <u>see</u> / seen a bald eagle flying overhead.
2. I seen / <u>saw</u> a grizzly bear last summer.
3. I seen / <u>have seen</u> salmon swimming upstream.
4. I think I'll drank / <u>drink</u> lemonade with dinner tonight.
5. Yesterday, I drunk / <u>drank</u> a lot of water.
6. I <u>have drunk</u> / have drank kombucha before, and I like it.
7. I hope our fishing boat doesn't <u>sink</u> / sank today.
8. My canoe sinked / <u>sank</u> yesterday.
9. His boat <u>has sunk</u> / has sank a couple of times.
10. I <u>can drive</u> / can drove to your house.
11. Aunt Ruth drived / <u>drove</u> to Grammar World Theme Park.
12. We <u>have driven</u> / have drived to the zoo three or four times.
13. Watch me <u>swim</u> / swam underwater.
14. I swum / <u>swam</u> eight laps this morning.
15. I <u>have swum</u> / have swam for 16 years.
16. He says he can went / <u>can go</u> to the game with me.
17. He <u>went</u> / goed to the game on Saturday.
18. He <u>has gone</u> / has went home for the weekend.
19. Aunt Ruth <u>bought</u> / buyed a vulture at the pet store this morning.
20. She has boughten / <u>has bought</u> asparagus for seventeen days in a row.
21. I'm going to buy four apples today. I buyed / <u>bought</u> seven yesterday.
22. He <u>brought</u> / brang the stuffing for the turkey.
23. Aunt Ruth had brung / <u>had brought</u> the crayons and face paint for the party.
24. She has went / <u>has gone</u> back and forth on the issue all morning. I wish she would just go ahead and purchase the rhino.
25. Flocks of geese have flew / <u>have flown</u> south for the winter.

Lesson 5

Myself

Determine whether the -self usage in these sentences is correct (Yes or No).

1. (Y) I think I can eat the whole stack of blueberry pancakes myself!
2. (N) She is going to reward myself with a free pass to see the movie.
3. (N) When they arrive, we'll give themselves a drink of cold water.
4. (Y) We should be able to conjugate these verbs ourselves!
5. (Y) I think he, himself, should wrestle the gorilla.
6. (Y) I found the Benjamin Franklin Founding Fathers trading card all by myself.

7. (N) Wait a moment, and I'll give yourself directions to my house.
8. (Y) Frank and Ernest helped themselves to a few cookies.
9. (Y) You'll have to read the grammar book yourself.
10. (N) The Steinhausers are going to send out graduation ceremony invitations next week to both you and myself.
11. (Y) I, myself, personally believe that John, Paul, George, and Ringo can handle their concert-scheduling problems all by themselves.
12. (N) I believe that you and I can work together to prepare a wonderful dinner for themselves.
13. (Y) Our guests should be able to work together to prepare their own dinner themselves.
14. (N) The only two people at the workshop were Hidalgo and myself.
15. (N) The elderly couple was so friendly that, upon leaving, they gave ourselves a homemade rhubarb pie!
16. (N) The chef did not realize that I was standing right behind her; when she turned around, I startled her, and she dumped the entire bowl of whipped cream all over myself!
17. (N) Andy felt that I should focus on helping himself with tomorrow's math homework.
18. (N) I gave the truffles to my grandmother herself.

Lesson 6

Superlatives

Underline the erroneous comparatives and superlatives in the story below. Provide the corrections in the space after the end of each paragraph. Example:

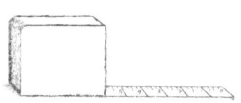

Of all the days I have lived—and I've lived many—this, by far, was the <u>happier</u> day. I found that I was gleeful; in fact, not only was I very gleeful, I was probably the <u>gleefulest</u> I had ever been. I would even go so far as to say I was giddy, definitely the giddiest I had ever been.   <u>happiest</u>,   <u>most gleeful</u>

1. What was the reason for this most joyful of days? If my tuba were to talk, it would tell you. This was the day that I reached my <u>higher</u> note ever; and this was the day on which I also reached my lowest note ever. That was the <u>excitingest</u> thing I've ever done.   <u>highest</u>,   <u>most exciting</u>

2. How does one get noise out of a tuba? If you have never played a brass instrument, it's not the <u>most easiest</u> thing to do. You can't just blow into a tuba mouthpiece as you would try to blow out a candle—that's the <u>ludicrousest</u> thing I've ever heard. Rather, you tighten your lips and then force air out through the lips, making a controlled air stream. To play higher notes, you need <u>the tightest</u> lips and <u>fastest</u> air; to play lower notes, you need looser lips and slower air.
   <u>easiest</u>,   <u>most ludicrous</u>,   <u>tighter</u>,   <u>faster</u>

3. Slower air does not mean less air. Lower notes require more air than higher notes. In fact, for beginning tuba players, playing a low note will make the player <u>dizziest</u> when compared to playing a high note. The tuba mouthpiece is the <u>bigger</u> of all the brass instrument mouthpieces; I've heard people say that putting your face against a tuba mouthpiece is like putting your face against a bathtub and trying to get noise out of it. That's a silly analogy, but it's a good visual.
       <u>dizzier</u>,   <u>biggest</u>

4. Playing the tuba is my <u>favoritist</u> hobby. I find a great amount of enjoyment in making nice music. And regardless of what the neighbors, the dogs and cats in the community, and the other people living in my house say, the sound coming out of a tuba doesn't have to be the <u>atrociousest</u> thing you've ever heard!
         <u>favorite</u>,   <u>most atrocious</u>

Lesson 7

An Honor, a Hawaiian

Circle any errors you find with the usage of articles a/an with words beginning with the letter H. Assume standard American pronunciation.

"What did you order for breakfast, Aunt Ruth?" I asked somewhat impatiently, not so much in <u>an hurry</u> as much as I was just frustrated at being late getting to the restaurant.

"I ordered <u>an ham</u> omelet," said my aunt. "What are you going to have?"

"I think I'll get <u>an Hawaiian</u> Surprise," I replied, taking one last glance at a handsome menu. "I'm assuming that comes with spices, maybe <u>a herb</u> or two."

"I remember picking an herb from your garden," said Aunt Ruth. "In fact, it was when you had that party with a horticulturist, a hawk, <u>an historical</u> book, <u>an hang-glider</u>, and a home run. That was an eclectic collection of H-words."

"Don't forget we had a hound dog, <u>an hurricane</u>, a harp, a handsaw, <u>an habanero</u> pepper, and a house."

"Oh, right."

"This is a weird story."

"It's okay. It might be <u>an hit</u> or a miss; the point is, keeping using H-words."

"Right. A Hampton Roads student may be reading this very sentence."

"Well, a Harrisonburg student may be reading it as well, and he/she may be doing so while riding a humble[1] donkey."

"I hope people read this carefully and not in <u>an haphazard</u> way."

"I read that riding a handcart around <u>an hairpin</u> curve can be <u>an harrowing</u> experience!"

"Well, I heard on the news about <u>a honorable</u> ballplayer who was also <u>a honest</u> man. He saw <u>an Hartford</u> fan drop a hat onto the field. He returned <u>an hat</u> to the fan, who then bought the player <u>an hot</u> dog."

"Looks like breakfast is ready! I wonder what's in a Hawaiian surprise?" The waiter set the tray on the table and removed the lid. In the middle of the plate was <u>an half</u>-eaten pineapple and <u>an hairy</u> hamster!

I turned to the waiter and asked, "Could I just have <u>an hard</u>-boiled egg instead? I'm not a hungry customer any more."

---

1   In the South, "humble" is sometimes pronounced with the unaspirated beginning. For those speakers, "an humble" is correct.

Review 2

Underline the correct verb.

1. I **gone** / <u>went</u> to the ballet yesterday.
2. I **have went** / <u>have gone</u> to the ballet before.
3. My friends Butch, Buster, and Gore <u>went</u> / **gone** to the opera last weekend.
4. Alyssa and Aria **have went** / <u>have gone</u> to the Monster Truck Extravaganza.

Decide whether the underlined superlatives are Correct (C) or Incorrect (I).

5. (I) Miss Tory is the <u>most nice</u> teacher you could expect to find anywhere.
6. (C) My tuba ensemble, on the other hand, has a <u>more enjoyable</u> sound.
7. (I) In my opinion, Beethoven was the <u>greater</u> of the world's composers.
8. (I) My brother, when compared with my sister, is the <u>tallest</u> of the two.
9. (I) Between choices A, B, and C, I would have to say that C is the <u>spicier</u> hot sauce.

Determine whether the -self words are Correct (C) or Incorrect (I).

10. (I) I don't think he can polish his tuba hisself.
11. (C) She can polish her trumpet herself.
12. (I) After you finish with the pencil sharpener, could you pass it to myself?
13. (C) I can't believe they finished the entire cake all by themselves!
14. (I) If it were up to themselves, they would have added a quart of ice cream too!
15. (C) I cooked an egg this morning all by myself.

Underline the H- words below that use the article "an" (i.e., the words that are not aspirated).

hammer	<u>hour</u>	horse	<u>heir</u>	hat
hopeful	hen	<u>herb</u>	<u>honest</u>	horror
handle	hit	hobby	happy	<u>honor</u>

Lesson 8

Bring and Take

Select the appropriate word.

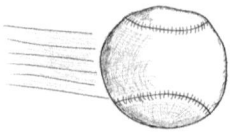

1. We have plenty of food leftover from the party. I hope that you will <u>take</u> / bring some of it home with you when you go.

2. The book binders are free. Be sure to <u>take</u> / bring one with you when you leave.

3. Could you stop by the store after work and take / <u>bring</u> home some ice cream to eat after dinner?

4. What food can I take / <u>bring</u> to your social tomorrow night?

5. Would that be okay with you if I were to take / <u>bring</u> my dog to your sister's birthday party?

6. I need the entire refrigerator emptied by tonight, so feel free to <u>take</u> / bring whatever you want.

7. I <u>brought</u> / brang exactly what she asked for—chocolate mints in the shape of Mount Rushmore—but she was still unhappy.

8. I have brung / <u>brought</u> eleven new customers into the grammar store in just the past two hours.

9. Why did you take / <u>bring</u> me here, Uncle Verne? It looks like the only thing you can do here is fish.

10. Why did you <u>take</u> / bring me away from my lunch? I was thoroughly enjoying the Mediterranean SPAM casserole.

11. If everyone in the club takes / <u>brings</u> a dollar to the next meeting, we'll have enough money to buy a chess set.

12. It seemed an eternity. At one point, I thought I'd never be able to escape. After just ten minutes at Aunt Ruth's apartment, she had me climbing the walls. I finally called a taxi to <u>take</u> / bring me from there.

13. The doctor said, "<u>Take</u> / bring two of these and call me in the morning."

14. Don't forget to <u>take</u> / bring your llama with you when you leave.

15. Don't forget to take / <u>bring</u> your llama home when you come!

Lesson 9

Used To

Circle any errors you find with the usage of use to or used to.

"Hey, you <u>use</u> to work in the motion picture industry, right?"

The voice startled me. I looked around the room and saw no one else. I am not <u>use</u> to hearing voices just out of the blue like that. At that moment, a movement in the corner of the room caught my eye. Standing there, staring straight at me, was a sheep.

"Baa, baa," said the sheep. "I repeat, didn't you use to work in the movies? In fact, I remember that we used to see you in the ads between flicks. You <u>use</u> to advertize for grammar products or something."

"I ... uh ... I believe you have me confused with someone else, perhaps my twin brother. I think he <u>use</u> to be in movies or pictures or something. At least, I remember that his picture did use to hang prominently on the wall at the post office."

"Your brother? Didn't he use to be the proverbial black sheep?"

"Yes, indeed. He used to be."

"So where is he now?"

"He's a used car salesman, a used book vendor, and the picker-upper person at the town park's reuse and ... uh ... recycle center." I had been looking at the sheep, but I wasn't <u>use</u> to chatting with a woolly quadruped. I quickly averted my eyes.

"Why are you being so sheepish?"

"I was going to ask you the same question."

"Well, my name is Eugenia; I'm a ewe, and that's why I'm sheepish. I'm a sheep. I always will be a sheep. And I <u>use</u> to be a sheep. That's just the way it is. Anyway, you can't pull the wool over my eyes. I am convinced that you are the guy, the one and the same, who <u>use</u> to do grammar commercials between movies."

"Curses, foiled again," I sighed. "I <u>use</u> to enjoy it. It even <u>use</u> to be fun. But how many times can you hear, 'Is he laying an egg?' without getting tired of it?"

"Are you really tired of it? It <u>use</u> to be fun. Can't it still be fun?"

"You know, you're right. I did use to really enjoy it, and actually I still do. I just needed something to write about in this story. That's the price of fame."

"Fame? Better get used to it, Buddy."

Lesson 10

Only Sentence Placement

Suppose you are on your way to see Mrs. Appleblossom, whom you enjoy visiting on a weekly basis. Suppose, too, that she is accustomed to sharing with you a pan of brownies every time you visit. Got that? Okay, now, suppose that you have an algebra test tomorrow and you need to study because you're still really confused as to why X can equal 7 one time and then equal 13 the next time. You calculate that you will have time to eat one brownie—no more, no less, just one. Between which two words in sentence #1 below should you place "only" so that you can accurately break the news to Mrs. Appleblossom? __eat__ and __one__

1. I'm sorry Mrs. Appleblossom, but I have time to eat one brownie today.

Suppose that you have a neighbor, Rowdy Roy Rawlings, and you enjoy fishing with him each month. You and he always prepare and eat the fish that you catch. Suppose, though, that this month when you fished, only Roy caught anything. You couldn't catch anything that day, not even a cold. Not only that, but Roy cleaned and prepared all the fish. However, you still joined him in eating the fish. Which sentence below best describes this paragraph? __3__

2. **Only** I ate the fish.
3. I **only** ate the fish.
4. I ate **only** the fish.
5. I ate the fish **only**.

If you ate the fish and Roy ate a hamburger instead, which would you say? __2__
If you ate the fish but did not eat the cauliflower or the spinach salad with lemon poppyseed dressing, which would you say? __4__

You and your sister Edna have been asked to paint the front porch. (I use "asked" loosely, for you and I both know that such requests are usually not optional if we wish our longevity on this planet to continue.) You, the epitome of responsibility, paint the porch and nothing but the porch. Edna, on the other hand, paints the porch, your dog Whitey (formerly called Fifi), and you. Between which two words in sentence #6 should you put "only" to best describe your role in this painting project? Underline those two words.

6. I <u>painted the</u> porch.

Lesson 11

Sentence Adverbs

There are several abuses of sentence adverbs on this page. See if you can find them all. You get bonus points if you can explain why they're wrong.

1. <u>Basically</u>, Marie Curie, the first woman to win the Nobel Prize, was the leading pioneer in the understanding of radioactivity. (Why? There was nothing basic about what Marie Curie did.)
2. Marie Curie, <u>basically</u>, was the first woman to win the Nobel Prize and was the leading pioneer in the understanding of radioactivity. (Why? Same as #1 ... *basically* is used as a sentence adverb here.)
3. <u>Honestly</u>, the thief took off with a king's ransom. (Why? How could the thief steal that much in an honest way?)
4. <u>Frankly</u>, the Houston Astros won the World Series. (Why? Does frankness have anything to do with baseball?)
5. <u>Truthfully</u>, it was the serpent that first deceived Eve. (Why? The serpent was absolutely not truthful.)
6. <u>Hopefully</u>, he will show up at the birthday party. (Why? What is he hopeful about by going to the party?)
7. He will play hopefully at the tournament. (Correct!)

8. The local newspaper frustrates me. <u>Specifically</u>, it is too vague on reporting the facts. (Why? What does it mean for facts to be vaguely reported in a specific way?)
9. What <u>specifically</u> frustrates me is that the local newspaper is too vague on reporting the facts. (Correct!)

10. Showing up in a white limousine with twelve dozen red roses, Artie <u>practically</u> swept Edna off her feet. (Why? There is nothing practical about how Artie wooed Edna.)
11. <u>Unfortunately</u>, it was Aunt Olga who purchased the Rembrandt painting for only fifty cents at the auction. (Why? I would say that Aunt Olga was most fortunate, not unfortunate.)
12. <u>Apparently</u>, the Invisible Man was here and we didn't even notice. (Why? If the Invisible Man were apparent, I think we would have seen him.)

Lesson 12

Metaphors and Similes

The English language is full of metaphors; most are obvious, but some are not. Some phrases that originally may have been metaphors are now considered so common that they are just part of the language. In the story below, circle as many metaphors as you can find. I see fifteen of them. How many did you find? Are there some that I missed? Remember, a simile is a metaphor too, so include them as well.

Aunt Ruth, a <u>bright star in the Grammar Universe</u>, sat <u>as quietly as a mouse</u>. She looked at me. I looked at her. She sighed. I sighed. Then, <u>quick as lightning</u>, she leaped out of her chair <u>like a cheetah</u> and roared, "We must reach a decision! We're <u>like a bunch of lemons</u> trying to decide if we should run off the side of the cliff and ...uh ... land in the cheesecake."

"I think you mean lemmings, not lemons," I suggested.

"Oh ... maybe that's why the waiter looked at me <u>like I have three eyes in my head</u> when I asked for a lemming in my iced tea."

"Did he bring it?"

"He sure did. That little critter splashed all the tea out of my glass <u>like he was doing the backstroke at the Olympic Games</u>."

"That's all very interesting, but it doesn't bring us closer to a decision."

"You're right. We're a couple of <u>bumps on a log</u>. We're <u>rocks in the field of life</u>. 'We're <u>slime on the shower curtain</u>."

"Slime on the shower curtain? What does that mean?"

"I'm not sure. We're <u>as indecisive as a peanut butter cup</u>. Are we <u>chocolate with peanut butter</u>, or are we <u>peanut butter with chocolate</u>?"

"Maybe we're a lemming cheesecake. Okay, we have to decide. On the count of three, yell out your preference. Okay?"

"Okay. Enough with being <u>marshmallows</u>. Let's decide."

"All right then ... here we go ... one ... two ... three!"

Aunt Ruth launched out of her chair <u>like a rocket</u> and yelled, "I vote yes to anchovies with our pizza!"

Lesson 13

Borrow, Lend, and Linking Verbs

Circle the correct word choices in the story below.

"Oh rats!" thought Anastasia. "I knew that Leonard shouldn't have borrowed / <u>loaned</u> his skates to me after I accidentally left mine in Tuscaloosa. The blades aren't sharp. I should have <u>borrowed</u> / loaned them from Amy. Still, the show must go on."

At that moment, Bill the Grammar Fairy appeared. "Excuse me, but you violated tournament rules by ending a sentence with a preposition. You should have used something like 'continue' instead of 'go on,' which is rather barbaric. My name is Bill, and I will borrow / <u>lend</u> you grammar advice while you perform."

"This is a skating competition, not a grammar festival," retorted Anastasia.

"Have you read the contest rules?" asked Bill. "Would you like me to borrow / <u>loan</u> you a copy?"

"Yes, please," she said. Bill handed her the rules. "The font is too small," she sighed. "Could I <u>borrow</u> / loan a set of glasses from you?" And moments later, she was handed a pair of bifocals. Sure enough, this was the World Championship Skating and Grammar Usage Tournament.

For each sentence, determine whether the underlined word is a linking verb.
1. (N) Isabella's dog <u>is</u> chasing the cat.
2. (Y) Zari's favorite pastime <u>is</u> chasing the cat.
3. (Y) The soup <u>tastes</u> funny today.
4. (N) Ada <u>tastes</u> the soup.
5. (Y) Darius <u>is</u> doubtful regarding Elon's ability to get there on time.
6. (Y) Igor's hobby <u>was</u> watching the mad scientist's patients squirm.
7. (N) My grandma <u>appeared</u> on a poster in the post office.
8. (Y) The Invisible Man <u>appears</u> to be late for his doctor appointment.
9. (N) Because the room is pitch black, Manny <u>feels</u> along the wall until he finds the light switch.
10. (Y) This assignment <u>feels</u> kind of strange to me.
11. (Y) My, you certainly <u>look</u> good today!
12. (Y) I think that chicken <u>looks</u> tougher than she really is.
13. (Y) This shirt seam <u>seems</u> to be unraveling.
14. (Y) Hello? Yes, this <u>is</u> he.

Review 3

Select the appropriate word in bold.

1. I use / <u>used</u> to enjoy singing until I heard a recording of myself and realized that a dozen hyenas have nothing on me.
2. Tomas use / <u>used</u> to absolutely loathe sauerkraut, but he loves it now.
3. Camila did <u>use</u> / used to dislike sauerkraut too.
4. Mr. and Mrs. Crayfish use / <u>used</u> to live one block over from their new place.
5. Is it true that the queen did <u>use</u> / used to visit you monthly for cooking lessons?
6. Could you please <u>bring</u> / take some peanut butter when you come?
7. Don't forget to bring / <u>take</u> the leftover elephant stew with you when you go.
8. I would not borrow / <u>lend</u> him your comb; I doubt he would ever part with it.
9. Your hair is disastrous; allow me to borrow / <u>lend</u> you a comb.
10. The smoky aroma emanating from the barbecue restaurant kitchen and wafting throughout the dining area was something that we could bring / <u>take</u> with us on our way out.

Underline the metaphors in the following sentences.

11. <u>Like a herd of sheep</u>, the mass of people slowly moved through the crowded hotel lobby.

    Is this metaphor also a simile? (Y)

12. From the moment she got up until she went to bed at night, Daniela was running non-stop through her lists of tasks; she was <u>the washing machine stuck in a never-ending spin cycle</u>; she was <u>the computer whose CPU was always pegged at max capacity</u>.

    Are any of these metaphors also similes? (N)

13. A birthday card from Aunt Ruth was <u>the perfect medicine</u> for <u>washing away the blues</u>.

    Are any of these metaphors also similes? (N)

14. Aunt Ruth is <u>like a goofy monkey</u> sometimes.

    Is this metaphor also a simile? (Y)

Lesson 14

Adjectives and Adverbs

Some adjectives are okay to use as adverbs; however, most are not. In the paragraphs below, determine whether the underlined word is being used as an adjective (ADJ) or adverb (ADV).

1. In the Really Old Senior Volleyball Tournament, Mrs. Bagsby served <u>deep</u> (ADV) into the opponent's court time and time again.

2. Close the door <u>tight</u> (ADV) when you come in.

3. There's food on the table for you, but there's no need to eat <u>fast</u> (ADV) since we're not in a hurry.

4. Run <u>slow</u> (ADV), Grandpa! Otherwise, Grandma won't be able to catch us.

5. Uncle Abner's rendition of the Rachmaninoff piece was absolutely <u>brilliant.</u> (ADJ)

6. To whom did Hercules turn for help when he encountered a jar with a lid that was too <u>tight</u>? (ADJ)

7. This morning I ran a marathon, auditioned for the local symphony orchestra, and hand-washed twenty cars at a charity fund-raising event; I think I'll take it <u>easy</u> (ADV) tonight.

8. Go <u>deep</u> (ADV), Grandpa. I'm going to hit the ball a long way.

9. Hey Noel, did you see how <u>deep</u> (ADJ) the snow is today?

10. That kid can sure hit the baseball <u>hard</u>. (ADV)

11. I know that you <u>deeply</u> (ADV) feel the need to finish your homework.

12. The homemade candy is tasty but it's too <u>hard</u> (ADJ) to chew.

Lesson 15

Verbs Ending in -t

Some verbs have a past tense form that can end in either -ed or -t. In the story below, identify the verbs that use an incorrect ending.

"Highly unusual, highly unusual!" <u>exclaimt</u> Aunt Ruth. "The situation is highly unusual!"

"Why, what's the matter?" I <u>askt</u>.

"Well," she began, "last night, while I <u>sleeped</u>, I dreamt about food, and when I awoke this morning, I was hungry. I had a hankering for an egg, lightly poached and with a light sprinkle of salt and black pepper. If I'm having an egg, lightly poached and with a light sprinkle of salt and black pepper, I reasoned, then I should also have a savory slice of bacon. If I'm having a savory slice of bacon, I reasoned, then I should also have a tart, crisp, green apple. If I'm having a tart, crisp, green apple, I <u>reasont</u>, then I should also have a round of fresh cheese. The cheddar that I <u>pullt</u> out of the fridge had spoilt, but I found a nice brie. I <u>gathert</u> everything and began cooking."

"Sounds like a great breakfast," I said.

"Yep," she replied, "but then I <u>lookt</u> down and saw how dirty the floor was, and I decided that the floor <u>need't</u> to be <u>sweeped</u>, so I <u>searcht</u> for the broom. I <u>leaved</u> the room, intending to be gone only a moment. There, in the closet where I have <u>keeped</u> the broom for years, I found a letter I had <u>losed</u> that was <u>sended</u> to me months ago by Uncle Worcester."

"Uncle Worcester, the relative who was so <u>bended</u> on becoming a leprechaun?"

"The same," she replied. "Anyway, I got distracted reading the letter and forgot about the food until I smelt the smoke."

"The smoke? Oh my!" I commiserated.

"Tell me about it," she lamented. "The egg had burnt; the bacon had burnt; the apple had burnt; the cheese had burnt. Everything had burnt!"

"Wait—how had the apple and cheese burnt?"

"There's something I've learnt[1] over all these years."

"What's that?"

"Aunt Ruth stories and drills shouldn't be over-<u>analyzt</u>!"

---

[1] The past tense *learnt* (a variation of *learned*) is not mentioned in the book but is a real word.

Lesson 16

Double Negatives

Read the following paragraphs and answer the questions below.

Aunt Ruth is planning a picnic for lunch on Friday. She wants good weather and she wants good food. Specifically, she wants no rain and she wants chocolate. She checks the news to find out the weather forecast.

The newsperson said, "We will have no rain on Thursday; but we are not going to have 'no rain' on Friday; and on Saturday we are not going to not have 'no rain.'"

Assuming the forecast is accurate, on which of the days below will it rain?

1. (N) Thursday
2. (Y) Friday
3. (N) Saturday

4. What is a more straight-forward way of saying, "We are not going to have 'no rain' on Friday?" **We are going to have rain on Friday.**

5. Can you think of two ways of saying, "We are not going to not have 'no rain' on Saturday," that are more straight-forward?
   We will have no rain on Saturday.
   We will not have rain on Saturday.

Now, regarding chocolate ... suppose Aunt Ruth demands that there be dark chocolate at the picnic. She also says, "I want to have no soda at the picnic." Suppose also that she doesn't want to not have milk chocolate at the picnic.

6. Which, if any, of the food items are required for the picnic?
   dark chocolate

7. Which, if any, of the food items are strictly excluded from the picnic?
   soda

8. Challenge: Try to explain why milk chocolate is allowed but not required for the picnic? **This is tricky. The phrase "want to not have milk chocolate" means the same thing as "want to have no milk chocolate," i.e., milk chocolate is banned from the picnic. But the original phrase begins with "doesn't." Therefore, she doesn't want to ban milk chocolate. Thus, it is allowed, but not required.**

Lesson 17

Passed and Past

Select the correct words.

1. After the sun had gone down over the western mountains, the daylight quickly became a thing of the <u>past</u> / passed.

2. I don't know how she did it, but somehow she past / <u>passed</u> me between the grocery store and my house.

3. You've not liked broccoli in the <u>past</u> / passed, so why do you think tomorrow will be any different?

4. She meant to have past / <u>passed</u> the football to me, but somehow she overthrew it and the ball went <u>past</u> / passed me.

5. I know I used to be grumpy, but that's in the <u>past</u> / passed. I'm a cheerful old curmudgeon now.

6. Do you know if we have past / <u>passed</u> the deadline for the auditions for "Aunt Ruth: The Musical"?

7. Kezia past / <u>passed</u> the test!

8. Rafael past / <u>passed</u> me on the race track like I was standing still.

9. I didn't think that Drew could eat all that ice cream, but once he made it <u>past</u> / passed the halfway point, I knew he'd be successful.

10. Michael past / <u>passed</u> the ball for a 47-yard touchdown in Saturday's game.

Underline any past / passed errors you find in the sentences below.

11. In the <u>passed</u>, we think about the future. In the future, we think about the <u>passed</u>, specifically how time has <u>past</u>. But we're past that now.

12. Ricky passed the basketball to Lamar. Lamar <u>past</u> the basketball to Henry. Henry passed the basketball to Shanique; and Shanique <u>past</u> the ball back to Ricky.

13. She passed me while I was driving on the Blue Ridge Parkway. I had seen the parkway in the past, though not for many years.

14. I told the officer that the truck had <u>past</u> me on the right, but he said that was a perfectly legal thing to do.

15. This is the last question on today's drills. Have I <u>past</u> the requirements?

Review 4

Determine whether the underlined words are linking verbs (Yes or No).

1. (Y) This <u>appears</u> to be an easy test so far!
2. (N) Lana <u>is</u> hoping that the test will be finished soon.
3. (N) The Invisible Man <u>appeared</u> before a live television audience yesterday!
4. (Y) Immelda <u>was</u> forlorn about the whole relationship.
5. (Y) Randy <u>felt</u> it was best to give her the cake before the ice cream.

Determine whether the underlined words are valid verbs (Yes or No).

6. (N) When the race car <u>turnt</u> the corner, it rode on two wheels for a few seconds!
7. (N) After the acrobat <u>jumpt</u> into the air, I closed my eyes.
8. (Y) After a day at the beach, I was <u>burnt</u> from head to bellybutton.
9. (Y) The snake <u>crept</u> along slowly, hoping no one would notice that it had stolen Aunt Mary's birthday cake.

Select the appropriate word below.

10. I want a piece of that cake so bad / <u>badly</u> I can almost taste it.
11. My knee was sore and I ran bad / <u>badly</u> at the race this morning.
12. I feel <u>bad</u> / badly about forgetting your party last night!
13. The soup we enjoyed last night tastes pretty <u>bad</u> / badly tonight.

Consider this sentence:

Is it not the case that you are not going to the zoo?

14. What is this question really asking?

    Are you going to the zoo?

Lesson 18

Numbers

Determine whether the numbers in the following sentences are written correctly (Yes or No).

1. (N) 7 is my favorite number.

2. (N) Wait, I thought 7 was my favorite number and fifteen was yours.

3. (Y) No, forty-four is your favorite number.

4. (N) 2147483647 is an important number on 32-bit computers.

4. (N) My dad is seventy-four inches tall.

5. (N) He hurled the shot-put four times and reached 51.3, 54, fifty-five, and 60.2 feet.

6. (Y) His grandmother hurled the shot-put four times and reached 55.1, 57.7, 60.0, and 62.5 feet.

7. (N) The boy finished 2nd in the spelling bee.

8. (Y) The bee finished first in the race to the flower.

9. (Y) The telescope was invented in the early 1600s.

10. (N) Not to be picky, but what you chose as your half of the pie is actually thirty-three sixty-fourths of it.

Lesson 19

Fragments

Underline the sentence fragments below.

I had a great time at the state fair. <u>This weekend</u>. The first thing I always do at our fair is to visit the 4-H building. <u>Arts and crafts all over the place</u>! <u>Homemade desserts</u>. <u>Paintings and photography</u>. <u>Even wood-working</u>! It's inspiring to see all the careful work that is done. <u>So creative</u>. Nearby, local vendors have booths where they sell big pickles at small prices. <u>Maple sugar cotton candy too</u>! <u>Pig races</u>. They are so much fun to watch. <u>Whew</u>! <u>Fragments all over the place</u>.

When I was growing up, I had a stamp collection. In fact, I still have it. <u>Stamps from all over the world</u>. I have stamps from places such as Tasmania, Sri Lanka, Myanmar, and Yugoslavia. <u>Bhutan also</u>! My favorite stamps are the old U.S. stamps. I even have a few that were printed in the late nineteenth century. I think my grandmother gave me those.

<u>Letters in the mail</u>? I still enjoy receiving mail (real mail, not just e-mail). Do you have a grandparent or an aunt or uncle or even just an elderly friend? I'll bet he or she would enjoy getting a letter. <u>From you</u>. If you can find a fun or out-of-the-ordinary stamp to use on the envelope, that would be great. <u>But, if not</u>. Any stamp will do, as long as it is enough to cover the postage cost.

We have a big garden. <u>A vegetable garden, where we enjoy growing a variety of vegetables and fruit, including my favorites: eggplant, tomatoes, and hot peppers. Okra too</u>. We also grow cucumbers—not my favorite, but my wife loves them.

Fruit. Our garden has some fruit as well. <u>With blueberries growing in the sun at one end of the garden and strawberries growing along the cool shade at the other end</u>. <u>Persimmons, too</u>. We have a persimmon tree that produces such sweet fruit. We also have grape vines. <u>Scuppernong grapes</u>. They're delicious!

We have discovered that humans are not the only mammals that appreciate good produce. <u>Deer, raccoons, rabbits, and possums</u>. The deer can jump an eight-foot-high fence; the raccoons and possums can climb the fence; and rabbits go under them. We have worked especially hard on the fence this year, and we have quite the barricade surrounding the garden now. <u>A virtual Fort Knox</u>.

<u>Fragments</u>! Try not to use them.

Lesson 20

Transitive Verbs

Determine whether the underlined verbs are transitive (T) or intransitive (I).

1. (I) Demarco's radio <u>played</u> in the background.
2. (T) Jayla's radio <u>played</u> Beethoven.
3. (I) Shaniqua <u>sang</u> as if there were no tomorrow.
4. (T) Demond <u>sang</u> "Tomorrow" as if there were no tomorrow.
5. (I) The hungry giant <u>ate</u> at 6:00 sharp.
6. (I) One character in Dickens' *Bleak House* spontaneously <u>combusted</u>!
7. (T) The owner <u>mailed</u> me the combination to the safe.
8. (T) The owner <u>mailed</u> the safe's combination to me.
9. (T) The quarterback <u>passed</u> the football to the receiver for a touchdown.
10. (I) The quarterback <u>passed</u> to the receiver for a touchdown.
11. (I) Ivonne <u>perspired</u> all afternoon.
12. (I) Hector <u>walked</u> from St. Paul to Tuscaloosa.
13. (T) Luis <u>walked</u> his dog from Boise to Seattle.
14. (I) Miguel sat in the restaurant and <u>ate</u> all morning.
15. (T) Beyonce sat in the restaurant and <u>ate</u> pancakes all morning.
16. (T) Ayana <u>cooked</u> a fabulous meal last night.
17. (I) Deion <u>programmed</u> all afternoon.
18. (T) Santiago <u>practiced</u> piano all week.
19. (I) Sofia <u>practiced</u> all week too.
20. (T) Alejandro <u>memorized</u> a twenty-minute speech in ten minutes.
21. (I) Mrs. Hernandez <u>slept</u> on her desk for the entire class period.
22. (I) Mateo <u>smiled</u> because his grilled chicken was a big hit.
23. (T) Valeria <u>attended</u> college this year.
24. (T) Uncle Julio <u>took</u> a test to get his engineering license.

Lesson 21

Active and Passive Verbs

Underline the main verb and determine whether the main verb is active (A) or passive (P).

1. The meatball <u>rolled</u> down the hill. (A)
2. The hamster <u>was seen</u> last by my cat. (P)
3. My cat <u>was seen</u> last by my dog. (P)
4. The bear <u>was laughing</u> at me. (A)
5. Samuel <u>wrote</u>. (A)
6. Mariana <u>wrote</u> a letter. (A)
7. My mother <u>was fed</u> by Diego. (P)
8. Luciana <u>fed</u> my mother the hamster. (A)
9. My mother <u>was fed</u> the hamster by Kayla. (P)
10. The pot of water <u>boiled</u> for over an hour before breakfast. (A)
11. Laura <u>boiled</u> the eggs in a pot of water before breakfast. (A)
12. My father <u>was eaten</u> by our big, overfed goldfish. (P)
13. The letter <u>was written</u> by Alex. (P)
14. Ashton <u>wrote</u> a scalding letter to the newspaper editors. (A)
15. I <u>scalded</u> the milk before adding the eggs, sugar, and vanilla. (A)
16. The milk <u>was scalded</u> as the first step in making ice cream. (P)
17. Scalded, the milk <u>intensified</u> the ice cream's flavor immensely. (A)
18. The robin on my porch <u>sang</u> a song this morning. (A)
19. A beautiful, melodious song <u>was sung</u> by a flock of finches in the yard. (P)
20. The eggs <u>were laid</u> on the table by the chef, much to everyone's surprise. (P)
21. The chickens <u>laid</u> the eggs on the table, much to the chef's surprise. (A)
22. The boy standing at the bottom of the hill <u>was flattened</u> by the meatball. (P)
23. The goldfish, overfed by my zealous siblings, <u>was eaten</u> by my father. (P)
24. The crowd <u>roared</u> when the team ran onto the field. (A)

Lesson 22

Intransitive Verbs Rule!

Underline the sentences below that use intransitive verbs.

1. <u>My dog drools.</u>   My dog eats apples.   <u>Mom sings.</u>
   Jimi plays guitar.   <u>My dog smells.</u>   A snake bit me.
   Mom bit the postman.   <u>Serena danced.</u>   <u>Marty smiled.</u>

Determine whether the underlined verb phrases are intransitive (Yes / No).
Hint 1: Linking verbs are intransitive.
Hint 2: Intransitive verbs do not have a passive voice (in other words, if you have a passive voice verb, it is not intransitive).

2. (Y) Bella <u>was</u> happy.
3. (Y) That magician <u>was</u> so good!
4. (Y) I <u>am running</u>.
5. (Y) Norma <u>ate</u>.
6. (N) Ronnie <u>ate</u> the hamburger.
7. (N) The hamburger <u>was eaten</u>. (*was eaten* is passive voice of transitive *eat*)
8. (Y) Nikki <u>will be</u> elated.
9. (Y) The mittens by the fireplace <u>were</u> warm.
10. (N) Gertie <u>is dribbling</u> the basketball.
11. (Y) I <u>am calling</u> to get tickets for the game. (no direct object)
12. (N) Kobe <u>was shouting</u> words of encouragement to Kara.
13. (N) The stockings <u>were hung</u> by the chimney with care. (passive voice)
14. (N) The fish <u>was caught</u>. (passive voice)
15. (N) Louise <u>was hitting</u> the target.
16. (N) The fireplace <u>was warming</u> the room efficiently.
17. (Y) That bruise <u>will be</u> purple tomorrow.
18. (Y) This <u>was</u> entirely coincidental.
19. (Y) The nuts <u>are</u> complimentary.
20. (N) Those nuts <u>are complimenting</u> you.

Lesson 23

Moods of Verbs

Are these sentences: indicative (A), imperative (B), or subjunctive (C)?

Example: Take that snake away from your sister! _B_

1. Uncle Raymond's stereo played Wagner all night. _A_
2. Run to the end zone, Cory! _B_
3. If Isabella were to sing, would you stay? _C_
4. If Daniela were to sing "Yesterday" tomorrow, when would it be? _C_
5. The handkerchief fell on the ground at 6:00 sharp. _A_
6. Edit this manuscript and have it ready by noon. _B_
7. Take the dog out before you watch the game. _B_
8. Did you hear that Aunt Ruth might run for president? _A_
9. Did you hear that the president might run for Aunt Ruth? _A_
10. Pass the ball! Pass it now! _B_
11. If Grandma were to sweat in public, she would be mortified. _C_
12. Deon walked from Boise to Davenport. _A_
13. Pick up your toys, Aria, before coming downstairs. _B_
14. They requested that she sing quietly. _C_
15. Kiana sang on her way to the lab. _A_
16. Throw the water balloon at Grandma! _B_
17. If she were queen, she wouldn't be peddling grammar books. _C_
18. Smile and say cheese. _B_
19. Put the cat out before coming to bed. _B_
20. Do you have a license to drive that thing? _A_

Lesson 24

Simple Past, Present, and Future Verb Tenses

Fill in the blanks.

1. What is the present participle of the verb *sing*? __singing__

Hint: What are you doing right now? I am ...

2. What is the past tense of the verb *sing*? __sang__

Hint: What did you do yesterday? Yesterday I ...

3. What is the past participle of the verb *sing*? __sung__

Hint: What have you done in the past? In the past, I have ...

Fill in the blanks with the correct form of the verb *eat*.

4. I will __eat__ food today.
5. In fact, I __eat__ almost everyday.
6. Corinne __eats__ everyday too.
7. Gene __eats__ on Thursdays when there's nothing else to do.
8. I __ate__ food yesterday.
9. They __ate__ food yesterday too.

Fill in the blanks below with the correct form of the verb *drink*.

10. You __drank__ a whole gallon of milk yesterday!
11. He usually __drinks__ a glass of milk before class.
12. She __drank__ all the orange juice we had! (Hint: note that there is no helper word here.)
13. I will __drink__ some prune juice with breakfast.
14. I know you don't believe me, but she really did __drink__ all the lemonade that was in the fridge.
15. We __drank__ vanilla custard last night.
16. I am going to __drink__ a tall glass of cold water when I get home.
17. The past participle of *drink* is __drunk__.

Lesson 25

Past Participles

For each verb, write the past tense and past participle.

verb	past tense	past participle
drink	drank	drunk
swim	swam	swum
sing	sang	sung
see	saw	seen
buy	bought	bought
go	went	gone
swing	swung	swung
bring	brought	brought
eat	ate	eaten
come	came	come
leave	left	left
rise	rose	risen
drive	drove	driven
fall	fell	fallen
run	ran	run
throw	threw	thrown
fly	flew	flown
teach	taught	taught
think	thought	thought
win	won	won
cast	cast	cast
cost	cost	cost
lose	lost	lost
ride	rode	ridden
sink	sank	sunk
grow	grew	grown
mow	mowed	mown

Lesson 26

Perfect and Progressive Verb Tenses

Underline all the verb tense errors you find below.

"Thanks for picking me up, Mom," I said, relieved that she <u>seen</u> me struggling with all I was carrying home and <u>choosed</u> to stop. I piled my tuba, my gym clothes, my basketball, seven textbooks, and the microscope I was borrowing from Mr. Hewitt into the back of the station wagon. I hopped into the front seat.

"No problem!" said Mom. "I <u>been</u> visiting Mrs. Green and the afternoon just <u>flied</u> by. You <u>knowed</u>, didn't you, that she's moving to Lincoln? She was so excited and she <u>sung</u> all afternoon."

"So what else did you do today?"

"Well, I <u>swum</u> at the Y this morning."

"You <u>swimmed</u>?"

"Yes! Then, I <u>gone</u> to the batting cage, picked up a bat, and I swung with all my might."

"You <u>swang</u> the bat?"

"Yes, I swung the bat!"

"Cool. What else did you do?"

"Well, today I <u>have went</u> to the store; I <u>have ate</u> lunch at the downtown cafe', and I <u>drived</u> to the library. Oh, before I <u>had goed</u> to the library, I <u>had ran</u> to the bakery to pick up Harold's cherry pie."

"Cherry pie! The bakery makes the best pies!"

"Yes, the pie looks scrumptious. You must <u>have saw</u> it when you <u>getted</u> into the car, though."

"No, I didn't see it. Where was it?"

"It was on the front seat, right where you <u>sitted</u>."

"I didn't <u>seen</u> it," I said.

It was then that I noticed I <u>be seated</u> on something wet and squishy.

My siblings sure weren't happy when they learned what happened to the planned dessert!

Review 5

Each sentence has one glaring error. Underline the error and write how to fix the sentence in the blank.

1. I won't say my car is slow, but I was <u>past</u> on the highway by a turtle that was walking backward.   **passed instead of past**
2. <u>1st</u>, make sure that you finish this test on time.   **First**
3. Matilda's kids are seventeen, <u>14</u>, and eleven years old.   **fourteen**
4. It took me <u>3</u> years to pass third grade!   **three**
5. Red, white, and blue cotton.   **This is a fragment! Add a verb.**

Are the underlined verbs Transitive or Intransitive?

6. (T) Grandpa <u>fried</u> the mushrooms on a skillet in the middle of January.
7. (I) Man, the sun was so hot that I <u>fried</u> out there.
8. (I) I <u>read</u> every night before going to sleep.
9. (T) I <u>read</u> a book about repairing bathroom sinks, and the next morning I woke up feeling really drained.

Fill in the table with the missing verb forms.

verb	past tense	past part.	present part.
see	saw	seen	seeing
eat	ate	eaten	eating
sing	sang	sung	singing
bring	brought	brought	bringing
swing	swung	swung	swinging
row	rowed	rowed	rowing
sink	sank	sunk	singing
drink	drank	drunk	drinking
think	thought	thought	thinking
swim	swam	swum	swimming

Lesson 27

Subjunctives

Select the appropriate verb in each sentence below.
Note that many of these are subjunctives.

1. Hamlet demanded that Polonius comes / <u>come</u> out from behind the curtain.
2. I think 2:00pm is when Polonius <u>comes</u> / come out from behind the curtain.
3. If I <u>were</u> / was to go to the store, is there anything you want me to get?
4. According to my calendar, this afternoon is when I were / <u>was</u> to go there.
5. I prefer that Aunt Ruth sings / <u>sing</u> quietly to herself.
6. I like it when Aunt Ruth <u>sings</u> / sing quietly to herself.
7. He <u>drinks</u> / drink the water in the green pitcher.
8. Ralph insisted that he drinks / <u>drink</u> the water in the green pitcher.
9. If a chocolate cake <u>were</u> / was to suddenly appear on my doorstep, I'd smile.
10. I had a dream that a chocolate cake were / <u>was</u> sitting on my doorstep.
11. If the team <u>were</u> / was to win every game this season, I'd cheer.
12. How did I know the team were / <u>was</u> to win every game this season?

This next section is tricky and not necessarily for the faint of heart.
Decide if the following sentences are subjunctive (Y) or not (N).

13. (Y) If they **were** at the game, they would have gotten soaked.
14. (Y) If you **were** seventeen, you could have gone to the "kids only" party.
15. (Y) If we **were** so old, why didn't they give us the senior discount!
16. (Y) The queen asks that we **play** trumpet in the style of Maynard Ferguson.
17. (N) The king observed that he **plays** trumpet in the style of Miles Davis.
18. (N) On sunnier days, he **goes** on picnics to Elderberry Park.
19. (Y) If the ship **were** on time, we'd have been there by now.
20. (Y) If the submarine **were** there, would this still be subjunctive?

Lesson 28

Bad and Badly

Determine whether the following examples of *bad* or *badly* are correct (Y) or incorrect (N).

1. (N) I sure feel badly about dropping the piano on Aunt Ruth.

2. (Y) Mike felt so bad about dropping the whole stringer of fish in the pond.

3. (N) I woke up this morning wanting so bad to eat a bowl of ice cream.

4. (Y) Nikita badly wanted to play Robert in a game of chess.

5. (Y) Robert wanted to play Nikita badly in a game of chess.
   (Note: Though this is poorly written (#4 is a better way to write it), the sentence is correct.)

6. (N) It's such a beautiful day after so many weeks of cold weather that I want bad to go out and run in the grass.

7. (N) Would it look badly if I went to the candy store instead of the funeral?

8. (N) I didn't want to tell you, but the shrimp in your fridge smells badly.

9. (Y) Your dog's breath smells rather bad today.

10. (Y) Aunt Ruth smells bad. I put a clothespin on her nose; now she also smells badly.

11. (Y) I removed the clothespin from Aunt Ruth's nose. Her nose works well, but she still smells bad.

12. (Y) Chocolate on my fingers; chocolate on my lips; chocolate on my breath; and all the chocolate in the Easter basket is gone. I know this looks bad.

13. (Y) Alison's fingers were totally numb from the snow, and she felt badly for at least fifteen minutes afterward.

14. (N) I wonder if Mr. Krook, from Dickens' *Bleak House*, felt badly moments before spontaneously combusting.

15. (N) I could use a glass of cold water so bad!

Lesson 29

Comma Splices and Sentence Fusion

Determine whether the comma (or lack of comma) in each sentence is correct. If the sentence is incorrect, rewrite it correctly.

1. The oranges are fresh and tangy, the apples are a bit mushy.

   Incorrect[1] (comma splice): The oranges are fresh and tangy, **and** the apples are a bit mushy.

2. The clouds are getting dark it looks like rain's coming.

   Incorrect (sentence fusion): The clouds are getting dark, **and** it looks like rain's coming.

3. We have one dog, and we don't have any cats. **(Correct)**

4. Marcia is running for office as president, Bert is running for exercise.

   Incorrect (comma splice): Marcia is running for president, **but** Bert is running for exercise.

5. Jarvis gave me the hamburger but ate the french fries. **(Correct)**

6. Manfred climbed the mountain, he shouted at the top of his lungs.

   Incorrect (comma splice): Manfred climbed the mountain, **and** he shouted at the top of his lungs.

7. Henry hit his 715th home run I saw it on television.

   Incorrect (sentence fusion): Henry hit his 715th home run, **and** I saw it on television.

8. My grandma saw Secretariat win the Kentucky Derby, and I saw it with her.
   Correct

9. The gorilla escaped from the zoo Grandpa dropped his ice cream cone.

   Incorrect (sentence fusion): The gorilla escaped from the zoo, **and** Grandpa dropped his ice cream cone.

10. One and one make two, but one and two make three. **(Correct)**

---

1 Answers will vary. Comma splice and sentence fusion errors may also be fixed by separating the independent clauses with a semi-colon or making them separate sentences.

Lesson 30

More Commas

Based on the rules and examples in the book, insert commas or semi-colons in the appropriate places in the sentences below.

1. Jack rode the sled down the hill and ate macaroni for lunch.
2. Jack rode the sled down the hill, and he ate macaroni for lunch.
3. I went to the store to buy figs and a hamster and washed my toes.
4. I went to the store to buy figs and a hamster, and I washed my toes.
5. June went to April's wedding in May but appeared in Julie's wedding in August.
6. June went to April's wedding in May, but she appeared in Julie's wedding in August.
7. With midnight fast approaching, Cinderella knew she had to get back to her carriage, or she would be toast.
8. In the light of the full moon, I couldn't tell the difference between Aunt Ruth and Santa Claus.
9. When properly tuned, an orchestra consisting solely of tubas can sound divine.
10. The runner-up of last year's community snowman contest was focused and ready even before the season's first snowflakes fell.
11. Mrs. Schooner, the lady whose dog can play *Moonlight Serenade* on the piano, was on a talk-show last night.
12. Rover, a dog whose master is learning to play the clarinet, howled at the moon all night.
13. I was going to go to the doctor this morning; however, I discovered that the reason I couldn't open my mouth was that my lips were stapled shut.
14. We should go to dinner and a movie; then, if you're not worn out, we can go home and conjugate verbs.
15. **Challenge**: Many say that the original Yankee Clipper was a swift sailing ship; others say that the Yankee Clipper was a nickname assigned to Joe Dimaggio, the great New York baseball player; but those "in the know" understand that the first Yankee Clipper was a barber in Massachusetts.

Lesson 31

Colons and Semi-colons

Use semi-colons to combine the following clauses into one sentence.

- This morning, I woke up at seven o'clock
- I walked the dog for two miles
- I ate eggs, bacon, and a grapefruit
- I did a load of laundry.

This morning, I woke up at seven o'clock; I walked the dog for two miles; I ate eggs, bacon, and a grapefruit; and I did a load of laundry.

Using colons and/or semi-colons, combine the lists into one sentence that describes what you ate for lunch.

- a leaf lettuce, tomato, and carrot salad
- roasted brussel sprouts in olive oil, balsamic vinegar, and garlic
- a grilled portobello mushroom topped with avocado, barbecue sauce, and bacon

For lunch I ate: a leaf lettuce, tomato, and carrot salad; roasted brussel sprouts in olive oil, balsamic vinegar, and garlic; and a grilled portobello mushroom topped with avocado, barbecue sauce, and bacon.

Combine these two independent clauses into one sentence where you are demonstrating that the second clause is an example of the first clause.

- Hobbies are a great way to help a child focus and develop an interest.
- When I was young, I began collecting stamps and baseball cards.

Hobbies are a great way to help a child focus and develop an interest: When I was young, I began collecting stamps and baseball cards.

Review 6

Choose the correct verb for these subjunctive sentences.

1. If Carlos <u>were</u> / was in trouble, whom do you think he would call first?
2. Gertrude commanded that Shelby dines / <u>dine</u> with them.
3. With the almond shortage, if I was / <u>were</u> a squirrel, I'd be going absolutely nuts right now.

Determine whether the punctuation in each sentence is Correct or Incorrect. (If Incorrect, the words surrounding the infraction are underlined below.)

4. (I) After I woke up this morning, I ate an <u>orange, and</u> then showered.
5. (I) We saw a movie this afternoon at matinee <u>prices, it</u> was great.
6. (I) When I was growing up, I had a dog named <u>Max he</u> was a good dog.
7. (C) After breakfast, I wrote a chapter for the new book and helped Mrs. Stottlemeyer with her yard work.
8. (C) It has been a very cold North Carolina winter; I sure am looking forward to spring.
9. (I) I don't mind the heat of <u>summer, my</u> favorite seasons in Carolina are fall and spring.
10. (C) My grandpa had a simple motto that he carried with him through life: Work hard and treat people fairly.
11. (C) Here's the list of what we need before the trip: from the grocery store, we need celery, carrots, and apples; from the hardware store, we need a flashlight, bug spray, and plastic rain gear; and from the gas station, we need gas, oil, and the air pressure of our tires checked.
12. (C) I just saw a motorcycle racing down the street; I'm pretty sure that it must have been Aunt Ruth.
13. (I) For her birthday, she received ballet <u>slippers, and</u> a slingshot.
14. (I) Noah brought more animals on the <u>arc, than</u> I can possibly list here.
15. (I) Mr. Holmes was reasonably sure that he knew how the crime had been <u>done, he</u> had no idea who the thief was.
16. (I) Though Mr. Holmes was reasonably sure that he knew how the crime had been <u>done he</u> had no idea who the thief was. **(The long relative clause at the front of the sentence demands a comma.)**

Lesson 32

Etc.

Determine whether the following examples of *etc* and other abbreviations are correct (C) or incorrect (I).

1. (I) So did you have a big breakfast with sliced grapefruit, hash browns, eggs, bacon, and etc.?

   (The *and* should not be there.)

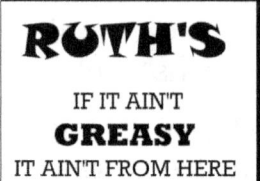

2. (I) My new dog does the normal doggy things, like bark, eat, sleep, scratch, sniff, etc..

   (Remove the period at the end.)

3. (C) I read in the course syllabus that this fall's class will include readings of: Chaucer, Spenser, Shakespeare, Milton, etc.

4. (C) Have you ever spent much time in Washington, D.C.?

5. (I) When I was in college, I spent a summer in Washington, D.C..

   (Remove the period at the end.)

6. (C) In 1927, Aunt Ruth took me to a Yankees game and I saw Babe Ruth, Lou Gehrig, etc.

7. (I) My dog was so embarrassed at being caught raiding the fridge that she turned every color of the rainbow: red, orange, and etc.

   (Remove the *and*.)

8. (C) My mom was so embarrassed at falling through the roof of the paint supply store and turning every color of the rainbow: violet, indigo, blue, green, yellow, orange, etc.

9. (C) I love these grammar lessons and I'm learning all about commas, verbs, how to use "etc.," etc.

Lesson 33

Either Or

Determine whether the uses of *either, neither, or,* and *nor* correctly match the verb forms in the sentences below (Correct or Incorrect).

1. (I) Sam or Janet are going to be there when the yacht is launched.
2. (I) Either of us are glad to be of assistance.
3. (C) Either of us is a likely candidate for the new position.
4. (C) Aunt Ruth or the boys are able to answer your questions.
5. (I) Either the boys or Ruth are going hiking on Saturday.
6. (C) Either the boys or Bob is able to go parachuting with you tomorrow.
7. (C) Either Ruth or Herman is the guest lecturer at the Denture Exchange on Monday.
8. (C) Neither Ronald nor the Bobbsie Twins have any intention of showing up at the meeting.
9. (C) Neither the Hardy Boys nor Nancy are available for comments.
10. (C) Someone once told me that neither money nor fame is going to buy you real happiness.
11. (C) Neither Abbott nor Costello has any idea how funny their material is!
12. (C) I don't know if Grandpa or the storms are going to get here first.
13. (C) I also don't know if the Joneses or Grandma is supposed to bring dessert for tonight's party.
14. (C) Neither of us is a likely candidate for the new position.
15. (I)[1] Neither the boys nor Bob is able to go parachuting with you tomorrow.
16. (C) Do you think that George or Thomas is going to appear on the first one-dollar bill?
17. (C) I know for certain that neither Benedict nor Aaron is going to be on any of the paper currency.
18. (C) Neither Frodo nor Sam was aware of how much danger they would encounter when they left the Shire.

---

1 Experts disagree as to whether *is* or *are* should be used here. Make it *Bob nor the boys are* ...

Lesson 34

Plurals

Next to each word below, write its plural.

1. antelope — antelope
2. sheep — sheep
3. fish — fish
4. rhinoceros — rhinoceroses (preferred), also rhinoceri
5. cactus — cactuses, also cacti
6. esophagus — esophagi
7. dog — dogs
8. hippopotamus — hippopotamuses (preferred), also hippopotami
9. crocodile — crocodiles
10. focus — foci
11. octopus — octopuses

BONUS! The book did not cover other forms of plurals, but it is helpful to keep these forms in mind. See how many you can get.

12. passerby — passersby
13. loaf — loaves
14. calf — calves
15. mouse — mice
16. goose — geese
17. wolf — wolves
18. life — lives
19. tooth — teeth
20. knife — knives
21. hoof — hooves
22. leaf — leaves

Lesson 35

That, Which, Who, and Double Subjects

Select the appropriate words to use in these sentences.

1. The black bear which / <u>that</u> ate all the food in our backpacks is sitting on the porch in a rocking chair.
2. The black bear, <u>which</u> / that is smaller than the grizzly we saw yesterday, is looking for more food.
3. My wife is the one <u>who</u> / that went to the theatre last night.
4. My dog is the one who / <u>that</u> went for a walk with me around the block.
5. Eggs <u>that</u> / which are hard-boiled are convenient for traveling.
6. Eggs, that / <u>which</u> are a great source of protein, are convenient for traveling.
7. I chose the pants <u>that</u> / which were blue.
8. I chose the hat, <u>which</u> / that was green.
9. Leonard's car, <u>which</u> / that really needs to be washed, is sitting at the far end of the parking lot.
10. The burgundy car which / <u>that</u> I want you to wash is sitting in the church parking lot.

Circle the double subjects in the sentences below.

11. <u>Uncle Carter he</u> is the one who gave me a whole page of stamps from Ecuador for my collection.
12. <u>Eleanor she</u> is the CEO of one of those newfangled high-tech startup companies in Silicon Valley.
13. Not to be deterred from reaching her goal, my <u>dog she</u> jumped over the cat and ran inside the house before Mrs. Barnes could stop her.
14. <u>Magic Johnson he</u> was one of my favorite basketball players back in the 80s.
15. One of the most dominant players in the game today, <u>Lebron James he</u> is pretty amazing.
16. With one of the strongest voices in the choir, <u>Floretta she</u> could shatter a crystal goblet from twenty feet away.

Lesson 36

Double Possessives

1. I have Aunt Ruth's photograph.

   This is an ambiguous sentence. Rewrite it so that it means:

   a) You have a picture of her.

   I have a photograph of ___Aunt Ruth___ .

   b) The picture I am holding belongs to Aunt Ruth.

   I have a photograph of ___Aunt Ruth's___ .

2. I am wearing a tie of my dad's.

   This is a legal double possessive. Rewrite it using only a single possessive.

   I am wearing ___my dad's tie___ .

3. I found doggy biscuit treats of my dog's in the backyard.

   The "of my dog's" is an incorrectly-used double possessive. Rewrite it using only a single possessive.

   I found ___my dog's doggy biscuit treats___ in the backyard.

4. I saw the collar of Gerald's cat's at the base of the flagpole.

   The "of Gerald's cat's" is an incorrectly-used double possessive. Rewrite it using only a single possessive. (This is tricky!)

   I saw ___Gerald's cat's collar___
   at the base of the flagpole.

5. When Vernon first began practicing, the sound of the violin's was absolutely atrocious.

   The "of the violin's" is an incorrectly-used double possessive. Rewrite it using only a single possessive.

   When Vernon first began practicing, ___the violin's sound___
   was absolutely atrocious.

Lesson 37

Nonplussed, Whoever

Are these uses of nonplussed Correct or Incorrect?

1. (Correct / <u>Incorrect</u>) After the earthquake, she was cool as a cucumber; she was the epitome of calm, the essence of serenity, and the pinnacle of peace. She, in fact, was **nonplussed**.

2. (<u>Correct</u> / Incorrect) Jack's day was anything but routine. First, he had a flat tire on the way to work; then, his dog texted him a message saying he was running away; and finally, his boss fired him. Jack was at risk of becoming **nonplussed**.

Select the appropriate word.

3. I think you should give the strawberry to whoever / <u>whomever</u> you want.

4. You said whomever / <u>whoever</u> gets there first can have it.

5. <u>Whoever</u> / Whomever received the package was one fortunate person.

6. The long pass was caught by <u>whoever</u> / whomever happened to be standing on the goal line at the time.

7. That man in the porpoise suit is the guy who / <u>whom</u> I had bumped into in Los Angeles last weekend.

8. Hey, that's the same fellow <u>who</u> /whom bit me on the nose this morning.

9. Ask not <u>who</u> / whom tolls the bell. I think it's Aunt Ruth.

10. I saw the horse who / whom / <u>that</u> won the derby!

11. I'll be happy to give the cheesecake to whoever / <u>whomever</u>.

12. I'll be happy to give the cheesecake to <u>whoever</u> / whomever wants it.

13. The beach umbrella was caught by whoever / <u>whomever</u> you happened to be sitting next to at the time.

14. Come out, come out, <u>whoever</u> / whomever you are.

15. Was that the same alligator who / whom / <u>that</u> bit you on the seventeenth fairway in last week's golf tournament?

16. The note said, "To whoever / <u>whomever</u> it may concern: I'm lost in a grammar sea, and all I see are ruthless waves ... ruthless, ruthless, ruthless waves!"

Lesson 38

Bored

Are the usages of *bored* Correct or Incorrect (C / I).

1. (C) After a week of unsuccessful shopping, Lucy was bored from looking for Christmas trees with Charlie.

2. (C) I get bored with something much more easily when I'm tired.

3. (C) I do not get bored by such invigorating activities as salmon fishing in Alaska!

4. (I) Is there anything that you get bored of during the day?

5. (C) The hole in the ear of corn, bored by the corn weevil, caused the corn to begin withering after a few days.

6. (I) Some people get bored of eating the same things at holiday dinners year after year. For me, the routine is very nice.

7. (C) There is a possum in our neighborhood that certainly must be bored by crossing the street in front of our house every night.

8. (C) The neighbor's dog must be bored from barking, every night, all night long.

9. (C) My grandmother once told me that a person with a creative mind is never bored with anything.

10. (C) Are you bored by this worksheet? It might be time to move on to something else.

Lesson 39

Ellipses

Determine whether the variations of the original quote are Correct (C) or Incorrect (I).

Original Quote: Beethoven, Bach, and Handel are great composers and are among my favorites. I would probably put George Gershwin right after them.

Examples:

(C) "Beethoven ... and Handel are great composers and are among my favorites."

(I) "Beethoven, Bach, and Handel are...among my favorites." (missing spaces)

1. (I) "Beethoven, Bach, and Handel are great composers and are among my favorites. ..."

2. (C) "Beethoven ... and Handel are great composers and are ... my favorites."

3. (C) "Beethoven, Bach, and Handel are ... among my favorites."

4. (C) "Beethoven, Bach, and Handel ... are among my favorites."

5. (I) "Beethoven, Bach, and Handel are great composers and are among my favorites.... [P]ut George Gershwin right after them."

6. (C) "Beethoven, Bach, and Handel are great composers and are among my favorites. ... [P]ut George Gershwin right after them."

7. (C) "Beethoven ... and Handel are great composers ...."

8. (C) "Beethoven, Bach, and Handel are great composers .... I would probably put George Gershwin right after them."

Lesson 40

Breath, Drier, and Lightning

Select the appropriate words below.

I visited Uncle Marvin last week in Savannah to help him install a new washer and drier / <u>dryer</u>. Reminiscing about the past, he told some funny stories and had me laughing so hard that at times I found it difficult to <u>breathe</u> / breath.

I hadn't been to his house in a long time, but I remembered that he had a fishing pond near his backyard. After Uncle Marvin went to sleep, I decided to fish for a few minutes. It had been reigning / <u>raining</u>, and there had been a lot of thunder and lightening / <u>lightning</u>. I decided to wear boots instead of sandals because I knew that boots would keep my feet dryer / <u>drier</u>.

The reign / <u>rain</u> picked up again as soon as I stepped outside, but I resolved to fish anyway. I took a deep <u>breath</u> / breathe and cast my hook as far as it could go. I waited patiently. A stiff breeze came, and I felt my line tug a little. I tugged back. This went on for quite a while. It seemed that every time I tugged, whatever was on the other end of the line would respond by tugging back. I was so excited that I ended up fishing all night.

Finally, dawn arrived and the sky began <u>lightening</u> / lightning. I was completely soaked from the reign / <u>rain</u> and couldn't wait to put my clothes into the <u>dryer</u> / drier. Now that I could see, I followed my fishing line and discovered that I hadn't been fishing in water at all. My hook was in the neighbor's back yard, caught on laundry that had been <u>hung</u> / hanged on the clothes line. I thought about climbing over the neighbor's fence so that I could retrieve the hook, but that might be construed as trespassing, and I knew that criminals had been hung / <u>hanged</u> for less.

When I finally went back into the house, Uncle Marvin excitedly asked me, "How was fishing? What did you catch? Did you catch anything? Did you catch anything? What did you catch?"

"Calm down, Uncle Marvin," I said. "Relax. <u>Breathe</u> / breath. Count to ten. Now, take a deep breathe / <u>breath</u> and let it out slowly. Okay. Now, about fishing ... well, I didn't catch anything for breakfast. All I caught was a pair of Mrs. Johnson's underwear."

"Oh, too bad. Did you keep it?"

"No. When Mrs. Johnson came out, she said I couldn't keep it; but she did <u>loosen</u> / losen the hook for me!"

Lesson 41

Antonyms and Homonyms

Find the homonym pairs in the sentences below.

Example: After the wedding, the <u>groom</u> used a brush to <u>groom</u> his horse.

1. Even though the sky was sunny and <u>blue</u>, Jorge felt sad and <u>blue</u>.
2. Even though she was <u>green</u> and inexperienced, Maya hit the golf ball onto the putting <u>green</u> with impressive accuracy.
3. The weather looks <u>fair</u>, so perhaps we should go to the state <u>fair</u> today!
4. Though he usually ran hard with his <u>dog</u> in the mornings, Alejandro didn't feel well and decided to just <u>dog</u> it.
5. Even though she had enough water balloons to <u>arm</u> an entire platoon, she could only carry four balloons in each <u>arm</u>.

Find the homophone pairs in the sentences below.

6. He has <u>seen</u> the play a dozen times and knows every <u>scene</u> by heart.
7. He <u>led</u> in the fish contest even though he wasn't using <u>lead</u> weights.
8. We <u>read</u> a book last night—not the green one but the <u>red</u> one.
9. Etta, the queen who <u>reigned</u> last year, couldn't come to the parade because it <u>rained</u> all morning.

Identify the word pairs that are antonyms.

big / large	soft / fluffy	<u>smooth / rough</u>
<u>big / small</u>	<u>loud / quiet</u>	small / smaller
green / seven	<u>rude / polite</u>	<u>tall / short</u>
<u>dark / light</u>	<u>sad / happy</u>	<u>slow / fast</u>

Write a sentence that uses the word "play" in two different ways, demonstrating that this word is a homonym.

Answers will vary, but an example is:

Fred wanted to **play** outside, but he had to watch the Shakespeare **play** first.

Review 7

Select the appropriate word.

1. The car which / <u>that</u> I drove in college was a '75 Dodge Dart.
2. The red flag, <u>which</u> / that I took down yesterday, was of my alma mater.
3. Despite the fact that Jarvis had a horrific day, he remained cool, calm, and stable; he was / <u>was not</u> nonplussed.
4. If whomever / <u>whoever</u> wants to go to the museum tomorrow would raise a hand, I'll know how many tickets to order.
5. Feel free to give the leftover ice cream to <u>whomever</u> / whoever you want.
6. Ask not for <u>whom</u> / who the bell tolls; it tolls for Aunt Ruth!
7. All you have to do is give the blue ribbon to whomever / <u>whoever</u> you think is most deserving of winning.

Are ellipses used correctly or incorrectly (C / I) to shorten the quote below?

"My favorite writers include Tolkien, C.S. Lewis, Ray Bradbury, Robert Penn Warren, Poe, Clemens, O'Henry, and Shakespeare. They cover a wide range of literature."

8. (C) "My favorite writers include Tolkien ... Bradbury ... and Shakespeare."
9. (C) "My favorite writers ... cover a wide range of literature."
10. (I) "My favorite writers ... Poe ... and Shakespeare. ... cover a wide range of literature."
11. (I) "My favorite writers include C.S. Lewis, Robert Penn Warren, Clemens ...."

For each word below, write a sentence that uses the word in two different ways to demonstrate that the word can be a homonym. (Answers will vary.)

12. duck

The duck, not wanting to eat in public, decided to duck behind the curtain.

13. light

Light from the sun warmed the campground while Tom cooked a light breakfast.

Lesson 42

Got

Do the sentences below use *get* correctly (C / I)?

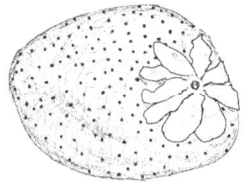

1. (C) I think I will get Aunt Ruth a new gnu for her birthday.
2. (C) Aunt Ruth got a new gnu for her birthday.
3. (I) I have gotten her some fresh, minty toothpaste in the past.
4. (C) I already got a hippo in the mail.
5. (C) No, thank you, I already have got a gnu of my own.
6. (I) I've gots three orders in for pizza tonight.
7. (I) I've gotten a letter in the mail every day this week.
8. (C) Has Aunt Ruth got a gnu already?
9. (C) Now she's got two new gnus! Who knew?
10. (I) Have you ever got to read the Magna Carta before?
11. (C) I wonder if Aunt Ruth got to know William Shakespeare.
12. (C) Did Aunt Ruth ever get to go to a college football game?
13. (C) Aunt Ruth got to look over Thomas Jefferson's shoulder as he penned the Declaration of Independence.
14. (C) Aunt Ruth has gotten to sing in Carnegie Hall. She was in the bathroom, second stall on the left.
15. (I) Aunt Ruth has somehow gotten two tickets to Tuesday's game in Madison Square Garden.
16. (I) You gots to be kidding!
17. (C) I have got to finish this worksheet before the game tonight!

What is perhaps a better way of writing #17 without using *got*?

I have to finish this worksheet before the game tonight!

Lesson 43

Possessives with Appositives

Answer each of the questions below.

Example: Harold threw away Mrs. Smythe, the friend who made the lasagna's paper plate.

    A) Who is Mrs. Smythe?
She is the friend who made the lasagna.

    B) Whom or what did Harold throw away?
Mrs. Smythe's paper plate

1. I roasted Agnus, the woman who liked to wear my mother's hats' chicken.

    A) Who is Agnus? She is the woman who liked to wear my mother's hats.

    B) Whom or what did I roast? Agnus's chicken

2. I accidentally left deep footprints in Lester, the guy who used to take us parachuting's garden.

    A) Who is Lester? Lester is the guy who used to take us parachuting.

    B) In whom or what did I accidentally leave deep footprints? Lester's garden

3. He bit Michelle, the woman who taught him how to make pizza's hand.

    A) Who is Michelle? She is the woman who taught him how to make pizza.

    B) Whom or what did he bite? Michelle's hand

4. Bob raced down the driveway on Julia, the neighbor with the yellow parakeet's red wagon.

    A) Who is Julia? She is the neighbor with the yellow parakeet.

    B) On whom or what did Bob race down the driveway? Julia's red wagon

5. After dinner, I washed my uncle, the one who used to think he was King Henry VIII's car.

    A) Which uncle? The uncle who used to think he was King Henry VIII.

    B) Whom or what did I wash? My uncle's car

Lesson 44

Let's, Less, and Fewer

Determine whether "Let" is used correctly (Yes or No).

1. (Y) Let's go watch them build the bridge.
2. (N) Let's, you and I, walk to the city market.
3. (Y) Let me walk to the zoo.
4. (Y) Let Rafael walk to the zoo.
5. (N) Let's you and I walk to the zoo.
6. (Y) Let us walk to the music store.
7. (Y) Let's walk to the music store.

Select the correct word to use below.

8. There is <u>less</u> / fewer water in the fish tank than there should be.
9. There is <u>less</u> / fewer rice in the pot than we usually have.
10. There is <u>less</u> / fewer money in my bank account than I would like.
11. There are less / <u>fewer</u> items in your grocery basket.
12. You can only use five or less / <u>fewer</u> coupons per day in that store.
13. Your diet would be healthier if you drank <u>less</u> / fewer soda.
14. Your diet would be healthier if you drank less / <u>fewer</u> cans of soda.
15. The drive from my house to yours is <u>less</u> / <u>fewer</u> than ten hours. (either is OK)
16. The number of fish in your aquarium is less / <u>smaller</u> than it used to be.
17. Kids, we'll be there in <u>less</u> / <u>fewer</u> than five hundred miles! (either is OK)
18. There is <u>less</u> / fewer sand on the beach today than was there yesterday.
19. The number of flowers in your garden is fewer / <u>smaller</u> than you have had in the past.
20. Occasionally I'll make such a bad mistake that I end up feeling like I have significantly <u>less</u> / fewer brains than a chicken!
21. With less / <u>fewer</u> ice cream cones than people, the party was about to end in disaster.

Lesson 45

A Veritable Cornucopia of Useful Information

Are the underlined words used correctly or incorrectly (C / I)?

1. (C) In the big parade, the marching band unfortunately was <u>preceded</u> by the cavalry horses.

2. (I) I think this workbook has kept you awake long enough. Please <u>precede</u> with your nap!

3. (I) <u>Beside</u> Leo, no one else thought that planting a lawn mower in the garden would really work.

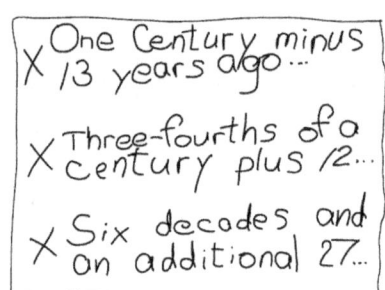

4. (C) Jade stood <u>beside</u> Aaron in his hour of greatest need as he struggled to choose between the vanilla and the chocolate ice cream.

5. (I) I have two tickets for the first game! I can't wait for the season to start. I've been <u>anxious</u> for it to begin all summer long.

6. (C) I haven't had enough time to study for the grammar test, and I'm kind of <u>anxious</u> about it.

7. (C) That girl is willing and <u>eager</u> to jump into any new project that comes along.

8. (I) Thunder, lightning, and a torrential downpour—do you really think it wise to scale the big water tower in these <u>averse</u> conditions?

9. (C) Though young at heart, I have become quite <u>averse</u> to cold weather!

10. (C) <u>While</u> Aunt Ruth is talking on the phone, she doesn't drive.

11. (I) <u>While</u> Uncle George had a sweet tooth, he didn't eat many desserts.

12. (I) It's a long <u>ways</u> from here to there and back again!

13. (I) Joel forgot to put eggs in the cheesecake; <u>plus</u>, he forgot all the cheese!

14. (I) When the cloned sheep looked in the mirror, he was <u>besides</u> himself.

15. (C) <u>Adverse</u> conditions in the universe can make a person averse, but is the converse true?

16. (I) Aunt Ruth went to the bowl game and was excited because the game was <u>proceeded</u> by a parade.

Review 8

Determine if the forms of *get* are being used correctly (Y / N).

1. (N) I have gotten three books at the library this week.
2. (Y) I certainly have got the rabbit by the tail!
3. (Y) Grandpa has gotten to sing at the Grand Old Opry music hall.
4. (Y) I got the rabbit at the animal shelter.
5. (N) He gots to be the guy for whom you are looking.
6. (Y) I get to go to the Bulls game tomorrow night!
7. (Y) Jane got to go to dinner with the governor last month.
8. (Y) That lucky girl has gotten to eat with every member of the Brady Bunch cast.
9. (Y) I've got to go see the new Aunt Ruth Grammar movie.
   (... but "I have to go see the new Aunt Ruth Grammar movie" is better.)

Determine whether these sentences using *Let's* are correct (Y / N).

10. (N) Let's us practice our tuba duets at 3:00 o'clock tomorrow.
11. (N) Let's you and I go to the store to get food for dinner.
12. (Y) Let's you and me go fishing at Jordan Lake this weekend.
13. (Y) Let's let lettuce remain on the sandwich.

14. I played my wife, the woman sitting across the room under the giant stuffed giraffe's harp last night.

    A) How is the wife described? **The woman sitting across the room under the giant stuffed giraffe**

    B) Whom or what did I play? **my wife's harp**

Select the appropriate word.

15. <u>Besides</u> / Beside Jerry, no one else was planning on going out for ice cream.
16. You can go to the game; I am adverse / <u>averse</u> to being in a large crowd this afternoon.

Comprehensive Review, Part 1

Chapter 1

Answer the following questions.

Birds like mosquitoes more than frogs.

1. With *than* as a conjunction, rewrite the sentence to make the meaning clearer.

    Birds like mosquitoes more than frogs do.

2. With *than* as a preposition, rewrite the sentence to make the meaning clearer.

    Birds like mosquitoes more than they like frogs.

Chapter 2

Select the appropriate words.

3. He turned the winning ticket <u>in to</u> / into claim the grand prize.

4. Ken was astounded when he saw Eileen walk in to / <u>into</u> the room.

5. The whole political situation surrounding the Watergate break-in cover-up turned in to / <u>into</u> a fiasco overnight.

Chapter 3

Underline the eight gerunds in the paragraph below.

Mr. McGonagle was thoroughly impressed with the daily buffet. The <u>baking</u> of the chicken was exquisitely executed; the <u>catching</u> and <u>grilling</u> of the salmon had been flawlessly performed; and the <u>roasting</u> of the brussel sprouts brought back vivid memories of <u>traveling</u> through Europe. The highlight of the evening, though, was the <u>preparing</u> of the desserts. When McGonagle joked with the waiter that he wished he could try them all, the waiter disappeared and returned two minutes later with a blender. The waiter then took all the desserts from the dessert tray and blended them all together. He handed McGonagle the blender and a very tall glass. The waiter said, "We take <u>joking</u> quite seriously here." From that moment, McGonagle has made <u>feasting</u> on the daily buffet his top daily priority.

Comprehensive Review, Part 2

Chapter 4

Choose the appropriate word.

1. Egbert was hoping to be there in time, but Norbert had already <u>gone</u> / went to the store before Egbert arrived.

2. Hobbes ran out into the street to find him, but in no direction could he find any trace. Calvin was <u>gone</u> / went.

3. Mortimer gone / <u>went</u> before his crazy but well-meaning aunts could persuade him to drink any of their ghastly elderberry concoction.

Chapter 5

Underline the incorrect -self words.

4. Can you read a book to <u>myself</u> before going to sleep tonight?

5. If they're hungry, they can get food from the pantry <u>theirselves</u>.

6. I myself can take care of the product registration.

7. Jasmine, you don't believe me? Look and see for yourself!

8. Alvin promised <u>myself</u> that he'd call me after the game finished.

Chapter 6

Underline the incorrect comparatives and superlatives.

That was the silliest movie I have ever seen. The movie's lead actor was cast in the <u>obnoxiousest</u> role, and the lead actress had the goofiest lines. The smallest character in the film would have been the <u>younger</u> of the three children. Two dogs—one black and one yellow—appeared in the opening scene. The <u>cutest</u> of the two was the black one. Overall, of the five home movies we've done, this was definitely not the <u>worse</u>.

For the words you underlined, write the correct words here (in any order):

    most obnoxious, youngest, cuter, worst

Comprehensive Review, Part 3

Chapter 7

Underline the errors you find with H- words below.

1. I had a harrowing experience while driving a harvester in a hurricane once.

2. It's <u>an historical</u> fact that <u>an humble</u> man can be successful as a horn player. **(Some from the South may pronounce** *humble* **with the unaspirated H.)**

3. <u>A honest</u> person is hard to find these days!

4. <u>An Hawaiian</u> vacation is near the top of most bucket lists.

5. Though giving <u>an Herculean</u> effort, the ant couldn't roll the marble up the ant hill.

Chapter 8

Select the appropriate word.

6. Could you be a dear and <u>bring</u> / take me a bottle of milk from the store?

7. Don't forget to bring / <u>take</u> tonight's leftovers with you when you leave here.

8. Larry, I'll see you when you come home. <u>Bring</u> / Take home your laundry.

9. Thanks for the book, Dori. Remind me to bring / <u>take</u> it with me when I go.

10. I should have bringed / brung / <u>brought</u> the instructions for the game!

Chapter 9

Underline the correct word you find in the word choices below.

11. Harvey use / <u>used</u> to play tuba in a local brass band.

12. He also use / <u>used</u> to play tuba in the university marching band.

13. People use / <u>used</u> to think that the tuba is not really a musical instrument, or at least not a solo instrument. And, well, people still think that.

14. In the past couple of decades, a lot of new solo music for the tuba has been written. Even before that, though, people did <u>use</u> / used to play tuba solos.

Comprehensive Review, Part 4

Chapter 10

It's a Saturday, and you've just spent most of the day riding horses at a nearby horse farm. You rode four different horses. On the brown chestnut horse, you trotted; on the gray horse you trotted and cantered; on the white horse you cantered; and on the black horse, you trotted, cantered, and galloped! Then, suppose someone asks you, "On which horses did you gallop today?" Using **only**, which of the following do you think is the clearest response? Circle your choice. **(C)**

A) **Only** I galloped on the black horse.

B) I **only** galloped on the black horse.

C) I galloped **only** on the black horse. **(correct)**

D) I galloped on the black horse **only**.

Chapter 11

Rewrite the following sentence, using some form of the word "hope," so that the unfortunate use of the sentence adverb can be avoided.

Nicholas said to Gabriella, "Hopefully, Aunt Ruth remembered to turn off the water faucet before she left the house."

Nicholas said to Gabriella, "I hope that Aunt Ruth remembered to turn off the water faucet before she left the house."

Chapter 12

The following examples each contain a metaphor. In any of the examples, is the metaphor also a simile (Yes or No)?

1. (Y) That bay has more sharks than a street lined with Chicago pawn shops.

2. (Y) That ballplayer has more bats than Count Dracula's family reunion!

3. (N) Shaking in his shoes but still determined to demand a salary increase from his boss, Stanley Sheepshaw stood outside and tentatively knocked on her door, hoping beyond hope that she wasn't there. She was. When she said, "Come in," he opened the door and entered, knowing that within two minutes he would be devoured by this cruel, corporate grizzly bear.

Chapter 13

Select the appropriate word.

1. Brianna, can you borrow / <u>lend</u> me your roller blades?

2. The chocolate icing on the birthday cake is melting. It looks <u>weird</u> / weirdly.

3. In an unfortunate mishap involving a cup of raisins, misunderstood instructions, and a rabbit cage, Morgan's cinnamon-raisin muffins smelled <u>strange</u> / strangely.

4. The master of ceremonies said that the prize would be awarded to both Georgette and <u>me</u> / I.

Chapter 14

Determine whether the following underlined adjectives are correctly being used as adverbs (Yes or No).

5. (Y) Don't make any sudden motion—just move nice and <u>easy</u>—and you won't alarm the snake.

6. (Y) Get there <u>quick</u>; the store closes in an hour!

7. (Y) You have to fish <u>deep</u> if you're going to catch a big halibut.

8. (N) You have to play <u>good</u> if you want to make it to Carnegie Hall.

Chapter 15

Determine whether the verb ending in -t is correct usage (Yes or No).

9. (Y) Last night, I dreamt that I was Aunt Ruth.

10. (Y) Eloise's request for promotion was ignored, swept under the rug.

11. (Y) She slept like there was no tomorrow.

12. (Y) I've learnt that you never want to have burnt bridges ... or is that britches?

Comprehensive Review, Part 6

Chapter 16

Suppose you want to go to the zoo. Suppose also that someone asks you, "Don't you want to go to the zoo?"

What is the best response so that you are clear and avoid any possibility of ambiguity? (C)

A) No

B) Yes

C) Yes, I really do want to go to the zoo! **(correct)**

D) Maybe

Chapter 17

Select the appropriate words.

On my way to work this morning, I was getting past / <u>passed</u> on my left and on my right by speedy drivers. In the <u>past</u> / passed, people didn't drive as fast. In the not-too-distant future, after time has past / <u>passed</u>, cars will be obsolete anyway—a thing of the <u>past</u> / passed. We'll all be flying around in jetpacks.

Chapter 18

Determine whether these sentences use numbers correctly (Yes or No).

1. (N) 2147483648 is not a good way to begin a sentence!

2. (N) I was 9 years old before I realized that the sun didn't drop into the Pacific Ocean at night.

3. (N) Jackie has four dogs at home, 3 cats, and two rabbits.

4. (Y) Of the fifty competitors, Bruce, Gary, and Thane finished first, second, and third respectively.

5. (Y) Hiding under the slide on the school playground, Karl ate 15/29 of the bag of candy.

Comprehensive Review, Part 7

Chapter 19

Underline the sentence fragments.

<u>Oh, that Charles Dickens!</u> I finally took the time to read one of his books that I've been intending for a long time to read. *Bleak House.* <u>What a wonderful book!</u> Once I started, I couldn't put it down. The book is written in two voices—one is the character Esther, and the other is a narrator. Dickens deftly used these voices to weave a thrilling story. By using more than one voice, Dickens was able to give the story a multi-dimensional feel, more depth than a single voice could provide.

Chapter 20

Are the underlined verbs transitive or intransitive?

1. (T) Malcolm <u>played</u> the organ Sunday morning.
2. (I) Linda <u>played</u> in the backyard Saturday afternoon.
3. (I) Ryan <u>sang</u> all morning while he was mowing the field.
4. (T) Hannah <u>sang</u> her favorite songs all afternoon while she was using the jack-hammer to break up the concrete basketball court.
5. (T) Addison <u>ate</u> the entire can of olives all by herself!
6. (I) Natalie <u>ate</u> all day long!

Chapter 21

Are the underlined verbs active or passive?

7. (A) Franklin <u>edited</u> the document this morning.
8. (P) The document <u>was edited</u> this afternoon.
9. (P) The chicken casserole <u>was cooked</u> by Nancy.
10. (A) Siobhan <u>cooked</u> the chicken casserole.

Comprehensive Review, Part 8

Chapter 22

Underline the intransitive verbs in the following paragraph.

On a beautiful Saturday morning recently, I <u>walked</u> to the new grocery store near our neighborhood. The store <u>was</u> about half-a-mile away, so the walk <u>was</u> pretty easy. At the store, I saw a lot of my favorite products on sale. I <u>smiled</u> when I saw them. I <u>danced</u>, and I sang a song. I bought several things, including a bag of apples. Later that day, one of the apples <u>tasted</u> funny to me. I took the apples back to the store, and they gave me a refund. I <u>am</u> happy.

Chapter 23

Determine if the following sentences are Indicative (IND), Imperative (IMP), or Subjunctive (SUB).

1. Are you going to the store today? <u>IND</u>
2. If they were going to the store, what would they buy? <u>SUB</u>
3. If I were going to the store, I would get broccoli. <u>SUB</u>
4. Go to the store and get me some broccoli. <u>IMP</u>
5. If he were going to the store, he certainly would get broccoli. <u>SUB</u>
6. Jacqueline is buying broccoli at the store this very moment. <u>IND</u>
7. Yesterday, Johnny bought a crate of broccoli at the store! <u>IND</u>

Chapter 24

Are these sentences simple present (P), simple past (PA), or simple future (F)?

8. (P) I sing in the shower every day.
9. (PA) I sang in the shower.
10. (F) I will sing in the shower.
11. (PA) I bought a singing dog at the music store.
12. (F) I am going to buy a trumpet-playing frog tomorrow.

Comprehensive Review, Part 9

Chapter 25

Select the correct word in each sentence.

1. Emma **has saw / has seen** an eagle flying above her house.
2. Have you **drank / drunk** the last of the milk?
3. Abigail **has swang / has swung** the bat hard tonight.
4. Chloe **has bought / has boughten** enough dental floss for all of us.

Chapter 26

Fill in the blanks with the correct form of the given verb.

5. By tomorrow night, I will have __sung__ the song. (Future Perfect of *sing*)
6. Next month, I will have been __running__ for ten years. (Future Perfect Progressive of *run*)
7. I had __seen__ twenty games in a row prior to Tuesday. (Past Perfect of *see*)
8. When I was sick, I was __drinking__ juice daily. (Past Progressive of *drink*)
9. Before I saw the cake, I had __eaten__ two cookies. (Past Perfect of *eat*)
10. I have __drunk__ iced tea already today. (Past Perfect of *drink*)
11. By the time I am twenty-five, I will have been __swimming__ for twenty years. (Future Perfect Progressive of *swim*)
12. By the time I am twenty-five, I will have __swum__ for twenty years. (Future Perfect of *swim*)

Fill in the blanks, supplying the helper verbs too!

13. I __have written__ for ten years. (Present Perfect of *write*)
14. I __have been eating__ it for ten years. (Present Perfect Progressive of *eat*)
15. I __had been singing__ songs. (Past Perfect Progressive of *sing*)
16. I __am swinging__ a bat. (Present Progressive of *swing*)

Comprehensive Review, Part 10

Chapter 27

Are the underlined words used subjunctively (Yes or No)? (Be careful!)

1. (Y) If he <u>were</u> king, why isn't he wearing a crown?
2. (Y) If they <u>were</u> royalty, wouldn't they behave better than they are?
3. (Y) Jane said, "I demand that Tarzan <u>come</u> down from the tree now!"
4. (N) They <u>were</u> in a rainstorm all afternoon.

Chapter 28

Underline the correct word.

5. Why are those senior citizens behaving so <u>badly</u> / bad?
6. Why does this soup smell so badly / <u>bad</u>?
7. I want so <u>badly</u> / bad to finish this test!

Chapter 29

The sentence below is an example of a comma splice. Name at least two things you could do to fix it.

    It's getting cold outside, you should start wearing shoes again.

You could replace the comma with a semi-colon; you could replace the comma with a period to make it two sentences; or you could add the conjunction "so" before "you" so that the two independent clauses are correctly joined.

Chapter 30

1. Molly, the neighbor's dog, loves chasing tennis balls.

Do we know the dog's name? Yes   Who is Molly? **the neighbor's dog**

2. Molly, the neighbor's dog loves chasing tennis balls.

Do we know the dog's name? No   Who is Molly? **we don't know**

Comprehensive Review, Part 11

Chapter 31

Are commas used correctly (Yes or No) in these three sentences?

1. (N) Madison has math in the morning, and English after lunch.
2. (Y) Olivia has economics (econ), history, and math in the morning.
3. (Y) Ava has econ in the morning and both English and speech after lunch.

Now combine these sentences in 1-2-3 order and change punctuation so that it all becomes just one sentence. (Hint: You will need to make use of semi-colons.)

Madison has math in the morning and English after lunch; Olivia has economics (econ), history, and math in the morning; and Ava has econ in the morning and both English and speech after lunch.

Chapter 32

Do these sentences use "etc." correctly (Yes or No)?

4. (Y) Our garden this year has all the standard produce that one might expect: tomatoes, peppers, peas, beans, carrots, okra, etc.
5. (N) The movie featured video clips of the recent American presidents, including Nixon, Ford, Reagan, and etc.

Chapter 33

Select the correct word in the sentences below.

I don't know if Carla or the penguin <u>is</u> / are going to get there first.

Do you think that Kayden or the twins is / <u>are</u> faster at rolling downhill?

We know that either Oliver or Charlie <u>is</u> / are going to finish first.

Neither Hilda nor Marie <u>has</u> / have any knowledge of the surprise party.

Comprehensive Review, Part 12

Chapter 34

What is the plural for each word below?

1. genius   <u>geniuses or genii</u>
2. focus   <u>foci</u>
3. sarcophagus   <u>sarcophagi</u>
4. cactus   <u>cactuses or cacti</u>

Chapter 35

Select the correct words in the sentences below.

5. That brown horse is the one who / <u>that</u> kicked me.
6. I thought Aunt Ruth was the one <u>who</u> / that kicked you.
7. I gave my condolences to the one <u>who</u> / that sat by Aunt Ruth on the subway.
8. He's the guy <u>who</u> / that gave Aunt Ruth a dozen roses for her birthday.
9. She's the cat who / <u>that</u> clawed Aunt Ruth's legs this morning.
10. She's the chef <u>who</u> / that makes the best cheesecake in the state.

Chapter 36

Answer the questions below, using as possible answers choices A, B, or C.

    A. This is my brother's painting.

    B. This is a painting of my brother.

    C. This is a painting of my brother's.

Which (A, B, or C) means: My brother owns this painting? <u>C</u>

Which (A, B, or C) means: The person in the painting is my brother? <u>B</u>

Comprehensive Review, Part 13

Choose the correct word in each sentence below.

Chapter 37

1. Keeping a positive, cheerful outlook even after learning she was a martian from outer space, Aunt Ruth stayed calm and was surprisingly nonplussed / <u>not nonplussed.</u>

2. You are going to give the baseball to who / <u>whom</u>?

3. Are you going to give the baseball to <u>whoever</u> / whomever gave it to you?

4. You should be able to send the carton of Aunt Ruth Grammar exercises to whoever / <u>whomever</u> you want.

Chapter 38

5. I could eat fresh fruit at every meal and not be bored of / <u>with</u> it.

6. Jan hears the same speech every day and is not bored of / <u>by</u> it.

7. Are you bored of / <u>from</u> doing the same thing, day in and day out?

Chapter 39

Determine whether the sentences use ellipses Correctly or Incorrectly.

"My older daughter had imaginary friends, including Dephilin, Dollar, Kingdess, Rabbity, Brenda, Michael, and Wota. They never said anything, nor did they eat much. They were always welcome."

8. (C) "My ... daughter had imaginary friends ... Dephilin, Dollar ... and Wota."

9. (C) "My older daughter had imaginary friends, including Dephilin .... They were always welcome."

10. (I) "My older daughter had imaginary friends, including Wota. ... They were always welcome."

11. (C) "My older daughter had imaginary friends, including ... Wota. ... They were always welcome."

Comprehensive Review, Part 14

Chapter 40

Select the appropriate word.

1. After you wash your clothes, you can either put them on the line to dry, or you can put them in the drier / <u>dryer</u>.
2. The ground is <u>drier</u> / dryer today than yesterday.
3. The thunder and lightening / <u>lightning</u> drove the dogs into a frenzy.
4. The pilot made Aunt Ruth get off the airplane, <u>lightening</u> / lightning the load.
5. Before you play a note on a tuba, you need to take a deep breathe / <u>breath</u>.

Chapter 41

Are these pairs homonyms (Yes or No)?

6. (N) blue / blew
7. (N) lead / led
8. (Y) green / green
9. (Y) fall / fall
10. (Y) hound / hound

Chapter 42

Are these valid uses of "got" (Yes or No)?

11. (Y) I just got a ticket for the first stagecoach out of this two-bit town.
12. (Y) I've got a notion that the Flintstones were responsible for this.
13. (Y) She has gotten used to the idea that there is no place like Nebraska.
14. (N) Please tell me—I gots to know!
15. (N) I have one scoop of ice cream, but Stephen gots seven!
16. (Y) I've gotten to watch my kids grow up to be smarter than me.

Comprehensive Review, Part 15

Chapter 43

Each sentence below is an example of what happens when a possessive and an appositive collide. For each, list A) the appositive, and B) the sentence without the appositive. For example:

I mowed Mrs. Picklebomb, the lady who had lunch with us last Easter's grass.

    A) the lady who had lunch with us last Easter

    B) I mowed Mrs. Picklebomb's grass.

1. I sold Aunt Ruth, the woman sitting in the corner with a strange look on her face's ukulele.

    A) the woman sitting in the corner with a strange look on her face

    B) I sold Aunt Ruth's ukulele.

2. Martha licked George, the man who was our first president's ice cream cone.

    A) the man who was our first president

    B) Martha licked George's ice cream cone.

Select the appropriate words.

Chapter 44

3. Let's you and I / <u>me</u> go find a gluten-free pizza somewhere.

4. There are less / <u>fewer</u> eggs in the carton than there were this morning.

5. You have <u>less</u> / fewer money in the bank than you did this morning.

Chapter 45

6. Although used to averse / <u>adverse</u> situations, the chief inspector was <u>averse</u> / adverse to getting involved in the grammar scandal.

7. <u>Preceding</u> / Proceeding each football game next season, the players will be reminded of the importance of good grammar on the field.